SPECIAL EDUCATION SERIES
Peter Knoblock, Editor

Achieving the Complete School:
Strategies for Effective Mainstreaming
Douglas Biklen
with Robert Bogdan, Dianne L. Ferguson,
Stanford J. Searl, Jr., and Steven J. Taylor

Classic Readings in Autism
Anne M. Donnellan, Editor

Stress in Childhood:
An Intervention Model for Teachers
and Other Professionals
Gaston E. Blom, Bruce D. Cheney,
and James E. Snoddy

Curriculum Decision Making
for Students with Severe Handicaps:
Policy and Practice
Dianne L. Ferguson

Community Integration for People
with Severe Disabilities
Steven J. Taylor, Douglas Biklen,
and James Knoll, Editors

Helping the Visually Impaired Child
with Developmental Problems:
Effective Practice in Home,
School, and Community
Sally M. Rogow

Progress Without Punishment:
Effective Approaches for Learners
with Behavior Problems
Anne M. Donnellan, Gary W. LaVigna,
Nanette Negri-Shoultz, and Lynette L. Fassbender

PROGRESS
WITHOUT
PUNISHMENT

Effective Approaches for Learners
with Behavior Problems

Anne M. Donnellan
Gary W. LaVigna
Nanette Negri-Shoultz
Lynette L. Fassbender

Teachers College, Columbia University
New York and London

Published by Teachers College Press, 1234 Amsterdam Avenue,
New York, NY 10027

Library of Congress Cataloging-in-Publication Data

Progress without punishment : effective approaches for learners with
    behavior problems / Anne M. Donnellan . . . [et al.].
       p.   cm. — (Special education series)
    Bibliography: p.
    Includes index.
    ISBN 0-8077-2911-6 (pbk.)
    1. Problem children — Education — United States.   2. Behavior
modification — United States.   3. Special education — United States.
I. Donnellan, Anne M., 1943–   . II. Series: Special education
series (New York, N.Y.)
LC4802.P76 1988
371.93 — dc19
                                                    88-14103
                                                    CIP

ISBN 0-8077-2911-6

Manufactured in the United States of America
93   92   91   90   89   2   3   4   5   6

Contents

Acknowledgments

Portions of our efforts to produce this book were funded by grants #G008430014 and #G008530101 from the U.S. Department of Education, Office of Special Education, to the University of Wisconsin's Center for Educational Research (WECR). We wish to acknowledge the leadership provided by the Assistant Secretary of Education, Mrs. Madeleine Will, and her colleagues in the effort to promote humane behavior management techniques; we would also like to thank the WCER staff for their unfailing encouragement and support.

The art in this volume is the work of Tod Fassbender, who, as artist, teacher, and wonderful friend, combines talent and sensitivity in all he does.

The inspiration for this book comes from our collaboration with many hundreds of learners with special needs, with their parents, and with professionals who, though too numerous to mention, are typified by all the talented individuals who helped to create the National Personnel Training Project for the National Society for Autistic Children (now the Autism Society of America). We especially wish to acknowledge the input of the following colleagues who have shared their knowledge with us: Mary Graczyk, Marsha Clark, Pat Mirenda, Rick Mesaros, Beverly Kilman, Tom Willis, Pat Juhrs, Marcie Smith, Frank Warren, Jeanne Connors, Ann Schensky, Charlotte Ahlgren, and Marie Ruiz. We would also like to thank Susan Kenniston for her help in editing this volume.

And, saving the best for last, we thank Darryl, Brenda, Mike, and Tod, as well as Ethan, Sebrina, Nathan, Grant, Ayndrea, David, Dina, Bill, and, of course, John Douglas, all of whom know better than we their enormous contribution to our work and our lives.

Introduction

During the past 15 years we have witnessed a radical change in attitudes about and services for individuals with special educational and developmental needs. Federal and state mandates, research-and-demonstration projects, and the civil rights movement have contributed to the present circumstances in which even the most disabled learners are entitled to appropriate services in the least restrictive environment. The clear focus is on deinstitutionalization; community integration; mainstreaming in the public schools; and the development of program options in heterogeneous, community-based, vocational, residential, and recreational settings. It is, in fact, the assumption behind all of our work that a positive and constructive program recognizes that all citizens, regardless of level of impairment, have the right to learn to live, work, and enjoy recreation in natural settings with their nonhandicapped peers and others.

This changed view of appropriate programming has created a special challenge for educators, program administrators, residential care providers, rehabilitation counselors, and vocational service personnel concerned with learners who present severe behavior problems. In the past, these learners have been relegated to the most artificial and restrictive settings until their behavior problems were "under control." This strategy has met with only limited success for a number of reasons. Often, for example, the behavior problems have worsened because such environments are not conducive to the development of alternative and more constructive behaviors. Moreover, the treatment decisions have seldom considered possible communicative functions of problem behaviors. Even when the individual's problems have been "fixed" successfully in restrictive environments, the treatment gains typically have been limited to the specialized setting. In part, this lack of generalization stems from a dependency on aversive procedures. We have known since the earliest days of operant research that punishment does not generalize very well.

For some learners generalization is difficult, regardless of the nature of the procedure used. In order to maintain the gains made in the artificial setting, typically the treatment must also take place in natural settings. All other issues of effectiveness, legality, and ethics aside, it is clear that many of the treatment options that were permissible behind closed doors are totally unacceptable in integrated community settings. Time-out booths, squirt bottles, shock sticks, and the like are neither available nor tolerable in supermarkets, bowling alleys, junior high schools, and office buildings. More than ever before, professionals, parents, and advocates are aware of the need to deal with problem behaviors in a manner that is both dignified and appropriate in integrated community settings.

Fortunately, there is a technology that is less intrusive in integrated community settings and has been demonstrated to be effective for managing even the most severe behavior problems. This nonaversive technology, along with its legal, administrative, ethical, and procedural rationale, is fully described and documented in *Alternatives to Punishment: Solving Behavior Problems with Non-aversive Strategies* (LaVigna & Donnellan, 1986), a book that presents the conceptual and empirical foundation for this topic.

In *Progress Without Punishment*, we attempt to present this less intrusive behavioral technology in a practical format for staff who work directly with individuals with serious behavior problems. Chapters 1 through 5 include an overview of positive programming options and behavioral and instructional techniques that we believe provide the appropriate context for behavior-change strategies. Readers unfamiliar with behavioral psychology are referred to several basic texts listed in the bibliography. In chapters 6 through 12 we present nonaversive behavioral techniques. We have attempted to avoid jargon and provide useful examples of successful strategies from the behavioral literature, from our own experience, and from the experience of the hundreds of professionals, paraprofessionals, and parents with whom we have worked.

Over the years we have found that, regardless of the severity of the behavior problems presented, most individuals would prefer not to punish learners who have handicaps. In cases where learners were punished, it was usually because the staff just did not know what else to do, and it has been what most of us experienced as part of our childhood discipline. In the past, many of these individuals who punished learners believed the myth that punishment is necessary for behavior change. This book, and all our work, is an attempt to debunk that myth and let it be known that there are other and, we believe, better ways. We have tried to provide to a wide audience the knowledge that ultimately the power to bring about long-term behavior change is not in the use of aversives but in a greater understanding of the individual learner and the creative utilization of nonaversive technology.

We recognize that in urgent and immediate situations, it may be necessary to use physical interventions or even force to prevent destruction to life and/or property. But it must be stressed that these should be performed in as neutral a way as possible, to avoid potentially countertherapeutic reinforcing or punitive effects. Moreover, these should be seen as emergency procedures, not substitutes for planned, systematic, nonaversive interventions. There are good resources in the bibliography on how to do crisis management, and readers are encouraged to become familiar with such techniques.

Two notes on language usage are in order here. First, we have chosen the word *learner* instead of *client* because it acknowledges that, like the rest of us, the individuals we serve are full participants rather than merely passive recipients in the learning process. Second, in an effort to avoid sexist language, we have used both feminine and masculine pronouns, alternating their usage in order to represent both genders in approximately equal proportion.

Our hope is that this work will contribute to a future in which all learners will be treated with dignity, in which *Progress Without Punishment* will be accepted as self-evident, and in which the use of aversive events in the management of problem behavior will have become a footnote in the history of human services.

PROGRESS WITHOUT PUNISHMENT

Effective Approaches for Learners
with Behavior Problems

1

Positive Programming

RATIONALE FOR POSITIVE PROGRAMMING

Most of our readers will be looking for positive programming options because they prefer to deal with even the most serious behavior challenges in a positive manner. Occasionally, even these readers will be faced with administrative, financial, or other constraints which appear to limit their options. Thus, to provide support on such occasions, we will briefly review several reasons why it is legally, procedurally, and ethically imperative that program staff understand and use positive management strategies within the context of a meaningful, chronological-age-appropriate, functional, community-based program.

Legal and Administrative Issues

Most learners who enter our programs are protected by a variety of legal and administrative regulations that can and should place severe limitations on the ability of professionals to punish problem behavior. By "punishment," we do not usually include standard classroom or household disciplinary actions such as requiring that work be completed before social time or that sloppy work be redone, even though these technically might be considered punishment. Even these techniques may be precluded legally and/or administratively if the disciplinary procedures result in learners having a restricted program or being singled out in a stigmatizing way. In general, we are concerned with certain behavior change techniques that often are used in classrooms and programs, whether systematically applied or not. These may include time out, fines, and other response-cost procedures, and the application of aversive events such as yells, slaps, long-term restraints, overcorrection, water mists, and the like. Depending upon the severity and intrusiveness of the interventions, as well as a number of other

1

complex factors, these kinds of procedures may raise serious legal and administrative questions.

All too often, whether because of lack of knowledge, lack of support, or other reasons, staff have been fired, have received negative publicity, and have even been sued because they used aversive procedures they thought were necessary and that were modeled for them by well-known professionals. As publicly funded professionals, most teachers and other program staff could be faced with civil and sometimes criminal sanctions due to their actions, regardless of good intentions. Staff typically obtain "informed consent" before using severe interventions. If, however, they are not able to demonstrate that nonaversive interventions have been systematically attempted, the signed consent forms may be meaningless. This is because the parents or guardians cannot give truly informed consent if they have not been fully informed about the available, less intrusive alternatives. Because of the complexity of such matters, many districts and regulatory agencies are refusing to allow the use of punishment. Whether or not you, our readers, are allowed to use punishment, we believe that you will find this book useful because most teachers and program staff would rather *not* punish, given an alternative.

Procedural Reasons for Avoiding Punishment

Our experience and that of many of our colleagues convinces us that there are a variety of interventions described in the literature that are as effective as punishment, with fewer problematic side effects. Among the side effects associated with punishment are that it frequently elicits aggression by the learner against staff and/or against self, that generalization is poor, and that continuation of the punishment is often required in order to avoid a return of the behavior to its previous strength. Further, as additional programs provide service for adults and adolescents, the aggression issue becomes more critical because of the size and strength of the learners. Moreover, the use of common aversive procedures such as time out and contingent spray mists has become essentially impossible in community-based programs due to the negative feedback from co-workers, neighbors, and other citizens. Conscientious staff unfamiliar with alternative strategies often feel forced to limit the educational and other experiences of the learner until the punishment procedures "control" or make the individual "ready" for the community. Unfortunately, the well-documented generalization problems associated with punishment often make such "readiness" only a remote possibility, commonly leading to staff frustration and unhappiness.

Unlike punishment, most of the procedures we are presenting have the added benefit of being "constructive"; that is, they teach something. Even those that do not, such as the differential reinforcement of other behavior (DRO) (see chapter 6) are emphasized as being most successful in the context of positive programming. This issue is so important that we believe many, if not most, procedures cannot be maximally effective unless used in the context of a meaningful and supportive program. Within such a context, staff engage a learner's cooperation in learning to behave more conventionally rather than trying to "control" the learner. We have seen extremely severe problems brought under rapid control through positive programming, with a concomitant increase in staff morale and sense of success.

Ethical Issues

There are, of course, complex ethical issues when any authority figure attempts to change another's behavior. When punishment is used, these issues become even more critical. Many of these concerns are beyond the scope of this book, but the bibliography includes several works that address these issues. We will address a few major points here.

Simply stated, the use of nonaversive interventions raises fewer ethical questions than does the use of aversive control procedures. For example, swearing and verbal threats are behaviors that are acceptable or not acceptable, depending upon the context or situation in which they are used. Societal, religious, personal, and other standards have relevance for the acceptability or nonacceptability of particular behaviors. Requiring that a behavior be eliminated involves imposing one's personal values on another. Therefore, to provide an incentive for an adolescent to *not* use threatening language during an entire week raises fewer ethical concerns than punishing him for that response. The fact is that there are no behaviors that can be seen as "absolutely unacceptable" under all circumstances and by all societies. Thus, any time we designate a behavior as one to be changed, we are, or should be, faced with an ethical question. To the extent that we are acting against the individual's personal choices, of course, the issues become even more critical. Thus, it is more ethically defensible to operate within the context of a positive and supportive program. Punishment, particularly as used in barren, isolated wards and programs, may never be justified.

A related question surrounds the function that the problem behavior serves for the individual. Most educators and service providers have had the experience of observing a person who uses aberrant means to "get attention," from pregnancy in a troubled adolescent to self-mutilation in a young child with a developmental disability. These behaviors may be terribly dangerous, but their function may be legitimate, as there is nothing objectively wrong with wanting attention. Recent studies have shown that even some of the most serious problem behaviors demonstrated by individuals with handicapping conditions can, in fact, serve a communicative function. That is, the act of head banging may be an expression of frustration, boredom, confusion, or any number of other communicative functions for which the individual has no conventional means of expression. If one recognizes the function, of course, it will be much easier to implement a nonaversive strategy for helping the learner control or change the behavior. The individual can be taught to signal for assistance, for example, or to request a break when a task has gone on too long. If the problem is confusion, often ecological interventions such as changing the presentation of the task or offering a concrete picture schedule can be effective in helping the individual stop even very difficult behavior. We have provided more examples of such strategies later in this chapter. Beyond these programmatic considerations, however, we believe that the practice of punishing a person for essentially doing her best to communicate some message creates ethical problems. They can be avoided if nonaversive procedures are employed to develop and strengthen the use of less aberrant communicative means.

Conclusion

Procedurally, it is obviously helpful to do an analysis of the communicative functions of the behaviors of concern before attempting an intervention. The following section includes questions that may be asked in such an assessment. There is usually some identifiable reason for a behavior; otherwise, why would a person do it? We maintain that to eliminate a problem behavior from the obviously limited repertoire of an individual, without attempting to identify the possible function of that behavior for that person, is unethical. Moreover, while it may be true that minor problem behaviors may justify only minor interventions, ethically, procedurally, and perhaps legally the opposite is not true. That is, simply because a behavior is serious does not mean it needs or deserves a punishment procedure.

Of course, punishment procedures sometimes work to suppress behaviors under certain conditions. Despite its popularity, however, punishment (even severe punishment such as shock) does *not* always work. On the other hand, positive alternatives also have been used successfully in dangerous situations. We suggest that, regardless of the severity of the problem, punishment is not defensible unless all reasonable alternatives, based on a full functional analysis, have first been attempted systematically and consistently. These include positive programming, alternative communicative systems, ecological manipulations, and other nonaversive behavior intervention procedures, such as those in this book. Given such an analysis and repertoire of alternatives, we suggest, in fact, that you will find punishment is *not* necessary.

FUNCTIONAL ANALYSIS

As noted earlier, we believe that in most situations it may not be defensible to eliminate or change behavior without first attempting a thorough functional analysis of the problem. This functional analysis is qualitatively different from an assessment that focuses on problem behavior solely as residing within an individual. A good functional analysis looks at the behavior in context and includes an assessment of the reinforcement history, contingencies and preferences, antecedent and consequent variables, and motivational and other potentiating factors that might be influencing the behavior; and it examines situational variables and stimulus conditions that might increase or decrease the likelihood of the behavior. Such an assessment leads one to ask questions about ecology, curriculum, instruction, and communication. Many of these issues are complex and require that staff have available to them a qualified professional who has experience in such analysis. This is not to imply that only highly credentialed professionals can or should attempt to analyze behavior. Rather, in the absence of such assistance, it may be difficult to defend a particular behavior-reduction strategy. (Citations on this topic are provided in the bibliography.) In this section we have included a number of general assessment questions, as well as questions about the environment, curriculum, instruction, and communication, all of which should provide clues to the factors that may be affecting the situation. These questions are followed by case examples showing nonaversive strategies that may be generated by the answers to these questions.

General Considerations

SAMPLE ASSESSMENT QUESTIONS

1. When, and under what circumstances (e.g., setting, staff, activity, time of day) is this behavior most likely to occur? When is it least likely to occur? Are there circumstances in which it never occurs? What are they?

2. Exactly what happens just before the behavior occurs? Just after the behavior occurs?
3. What happens on those occasions (days, weeks, weekends, evenings) when the problem behavior does not occur? What interventions have been tried? For how long? With what success? Why were they stopped? Why didn't they work?
4. What activities, objects, or events have been identified as reinforcing to the individual? Under what conditions are they available to the individual?
5. Why do you think the behavior occurs?
6. What plan do you think might work, if you had all the necessary resources to implement it?

STRATEGIES

- Nathan's parents had a difficult time handling his tantrums at home. With help from his teacher they asked the question, "What happens just before the behavior occurs?" They determined that the tantrums typically occurred when they wanted Nathan to get ready to go somewhere in a hurry. By making sure they always gave him enough time, or gave him help when time was short, they avoided the tantrums.
- Kim chewed on her fingers and sometimes her hands. This was particularly a problem at her cafeteria job. Her job coach was very concerned. A consultant asked the question, "Since you don't want her to do that, what happens when she doesn't do it?" The job coach's answer was, "Nothing." The coach simply began praising her for working and not chewing on her fingers, and the problem was eliminated.
- Art had recently moved out of an institution into a supervised apartment. Staff were concerned about the number of times Art hit his head with his own fist. When the psychologist asked them why they thought he was doing it, they guessed it was because he always wanted food. He never hit his head while he was preparing or eating food. Staff showed Art that he could get food whenever he wanted, and in 1 week his head hitting was almost eliminated. After 4 weeks, the number of times he went for food and the amount of food he ate declined to a more typical level and amount.

Environmental/Ecological Considerations

SAMPLE ASSESSMENT QUESTIONS

1. Does this client have the opportunity and/or skills to make choices that are reasonable for his age and ability?

2. Does he have freedom of movement? How often can he decide when he wants to eat; go to bed; get up; interact; and postpone or prolong an activity, an event, or an interaction? Are such options provided routinely and in a manner that promotes the development of necessary choice-making skills?

3. Does this learner have the opportunity to interact socially with non-handicapped peers and other citizens on a routine basis and in a manner that enables him to acquire such social skills?

4. What are the communicative, social, and general functioning skills of the individuals with whom he spends his instructional, vocational, and recreational time?

5. How often is positive physical contact available for this learner? Does he have a choice? What opportunities are available, and in what manner is it appropriate for him to express affection physically?

6. Is there a variety of things for the learner to do spontaneously, during breaks and leisure time, without depending on staff to provide them? Do staff provide such activities, when and as appropriate?

7. Do staff interact with the individual in a chronological-age-appropriate social manner? How often do staff interact with the learner? Do they do so only when giving instruction?

8. How many different kinds of environments does this learner have access to in a given day or week? Is instruction confined to one setting, or is he given frequent opportunities to learn chronological-age-appropriate and functional skills in a variety of natural environments?

9. How many years has he been in this environment? What are the opportunities for advancement, for learning new and higher-paying jobs, for moving on to other preferred vocational or residential settings?

10. With how many different staff members is he in contact in a day? With how many nonhandicapped peers? How often does this change? How is he informed of the change? Is the milieu one that is interesting, supportive, and acknowledges the individual's right to be treated with dignity and respect?

STRATEGIES

• George was a young man with severe disabilities who often self-stimulated at his job but who never self-stimulated in other settings. The vocational program staff discovered that he was affected by the fluorescent lights in the room. They were able to deal effectively with this high-rate behavior by giving George a baseball cap to wear in the presence of such lights. They then developed a program with which they taught him to carry his hat and to use it whenever light was bothering him.

- Jerry, a 9-year-old learner with severe cognitive impairments, was found to have very high rates of stereotypic behavior in certain learning environments. The behavior was very stigmatizing and interfered with his activities. His teacher analyzed his various environments and found that his stereotypic behavior went up markedly in crowded environments. At first they cut back his time in such settings, while they taught him some relaxation techniques and gradually reintroduced him to more crowded and complex settings.
- Patricia was a young adult with severe impairments, confined to a wheelchair. She came from a large family in which there was always a great deal of commotion and interesting activity. When she moved to a small group home in which the other residents were communicatively impaired like herself, she began to have serious mood swings, depression, and even, for the first time, violent behavior. The assessment of the situation showed that the young staff were overwhelmed with start-up tasks and unwittingly were ignoring Patricia and the other residents, except when instructing them or managing a problem. Additional help was obtained through college student volunteers. The volunteers were given specific instructions on social interaction with Patricia and her housemates, and she was taught and encouraged to wave them over to her when she wanted attention. Staff also developed more frequent and interesting programs for teaching the residents to function in their community.
- Karen and Phil, two teachers of students labeled autistic and severely handicapped, discovered that once they began to do nonschool instruction and community-based teaching, many problem behaviors they saw on school grounds were reduced to almost zero. They thought at first that they were looking at a "honeymoon effect." They later realized that most of the change was a result of the students having a more interesting environment in which to interact and more reinforcing and meaningful activities in which to engage.

Curricular/Programmatic Considerations

SAMPLE ASSESSMENT QUESTIONS

1. What kinds of task demands are being placed on this learner?
2. Does the individual like doing what she is asked to do? How does she let you know this?
3. Is the individual given a reasonable number of choices about what jobs she wants to do and when and how she wants to do them?
4. If left to choose freely, how would she spend her time?
5. Are the activities meaningful, chronological-age appropriate, and intrinsically motivating?

6. Are the tasks ones that are appropriate, given the individual's skill level and sensory and physical ability?
7. Are the activities long enough for the individual to see that she is accomplishing something, but not so long that they are unreasonably tedious for someone of this age and ability?
8. Does the program offer new options and activities based upon demonstration of successfully acquired skill sequences?

STRATEGIES

- John, a young man who is blind and has severe retardation, was being taught to wash windows. After being assisted on two windows he began resisting assistance and then refused to continue work. After an assessment of the situation, it was decided that the task was not appropriate, given his sensory impairment. He was given a new job that involved packaging equipment he could hold and feel, and he became a more willing worker.
- Mary was a very active young woman. In her free time she chose to shoot baskets, ride an exercise bike, jog, or walk. Her job coach was having difficulty getting her to stay on task at her job, where she did filing for a travel agency. There were few opportunities for her to move around on this job. The job coach decided the best alternative was to change Mary's job. She tried Mary out at a large plant that needed a courier to deliver parts to different departments all day. Mary had no problem staying on task at her new job.
- Dan worked at a print shop sorting and packing paper. His job coach put together a picture schedule for him and always placed his two breaks at the same time every morning and afternoon. About every 3 days or so he would have a major tantrum, sometimes becoming destructive. An analysis indicated he had few opportunities to make choices of any kind. His job coach began letting Dan choose his break time and the order in which he would do certain tasks, as well as make other appropriate decisions, and his tantrums decreased to no more than three a month. This rate was then further controlled and eventually eliminated through a differential schedule of reinforcement.

Instructional Considerations

SAMPLE ASSESSMENT QUESTIONS

1. Are staff given appropriate training on how to teach? Do they know how to give instruction in a manner that makes sense to this individual?

2. Have staff been given instruction on how to develop and implement appropriate instructional goals?
3. What level of compliance is demanded of this learner? Is this applied consistently by all staff? Do staff know how to assess whether he is actually being noncompliant, whether it is reasonable to expect him to comply in this manner and form, and whether he even understands what is expected of him in this situation?
4. Through which modalities does this individual learn best?
5. How does the learner know when he will be moving from one environment to another?
6. How does he know when an activity or job will end and what comes next?
7. Are staff aware of any unusual learning characteristics of this individual that may interfere with compliance? For example, is he very dependent on contextual cues? Does he need a concrete visual representation to understand what is coming next? Would it help if activities were arranged in such a way that he could see the effect of his work? Does he have object permanence; that is, does he know something still exists even though it is out of sight or sound? What does he understand about cause and effect?
8. Do staff have a reasonable knowledge of behavioral technology for instruction and positive behavior change? Do they have resources that they can routinely call upon to assist them when confronted with difficult or confusing situations?
9. Have staff been taught how to develop adaptations to prevent or preclude problems and to assist the learner in becoming independent on essential tasks?
10. Is the learning environment structured for maximum independence and participation, regardless of the disabilities of the learner?
11. Is the individual allowed, encouraged, and/or enabled to participate at least partially in activities?

STRATEGIES

- Jack was not making progress in learning to perform the daily living skills he needed in his new community residence. The consultants determined that Jack would learn more efficiently if a discrete-trial teaching format were used (see chapter 3). Three weeks later he was still not making progress. The consultant had not realized that the staff were not trained in how to conduct discrete-trial-format teaching.
- Sam, a 7-year-old with autism, had difficulty following the teacher's verbal directions. At first she thought he was being noncompliant. She

began pairing all her directions with dramatic gestures and found he was able to comply.

- Susan, a deaf-blind woman with moderate retardation, screamed each time an activity changed or she moved from one environment to another. Her teacher determined that she was confused by the transitions. Susan's screaming decreased dramatically when her teacher developed a tactile schedule book for her, in which each panel had an example of familiar objects from the activities and environments in which she participated.

- Bill, a moderately handicapped, 19-year-old verbally competent young man, was at risk for an institutional placement because of severe aggressive behavior. A functional analysis of the behavior revealed that Bill's aggression was related to anxiety aroused by his not knowing what activities were going to happen on a given day. Bill's parents and involved professionals had been irritated by Bill's constant, perseverative questioning. Historical records indicated a short-term memory problem. Bill's vocational teacher helped him develop a picture calendar of the day's and week's schedule. Over time he learned to change pictures when new activities were scheduled. Bill was taught to utilize the calendar whenever he seemed anxious or began to perseverate on questions.

- Ben, a charming young adult with moderate retardation, was occasionally having temper tantrums and aggressive outbursts at work. The situation was very confusing to everyone, as he was generally very amenable and enjoyed social interaction (which he did remarkably well). An interview with his parents and others revealed that they had learned to guess when he needed help by noticing whenever he would stop in the middle of what he was doing. Because family and friends were very helpful to him, Ben never learned to give verbal or nonverbal cues to request assistance. During assessment, to verify this, he was asked to do nonsense things, along with functional requests. For example, the teacher would say, "Pass the salt, please," and "Thanks" when the task was completed. Then he would say, "Now, would you raffle the snort?" Ben gave no sign of confusion other than stopping. Unfortunately, his job coach saw his stopping as noncompliance, and the confusion sometimes resulted in a major incident. The solution included gradually shaping communicative behaviors for Ben and teaching staff how to differentiate nonconventional communication from noncompliant behavior.

Communicative Functions

Researchers have demonstrated that many behaviors that appear odd and even dangerous may be the individual's best way of expressing something extremely important to her (Donnellan, Mirenda, Mesaros, & Fassbender, 1984; see "Positive Programming" section in the bibliography). This is particularly true for learners with handicaps, who may have few conventional ways of communicating, and for individuals who have no way of communicating under certain stressful situations. Obviously, an understanding of the learner's communication patterns will greatly facilitate efforts to engage the learner in behavior change. In addition to reviewing the answers generated by the assessment questions given previously, the following additional questions, designed to reveal further the communicative functions of the problem behavior, should be asked.

SAMPLE ASSESSMENT QUESTIONS

1. How might this learner be "interpreting" the situation?
2. If changing activities or going from one place to another is confusing for her, does she have the skill to express anxiety? Fear? Confusion? If in the past staff always told her to get the milk out of the refrigerator, perhaps she thinks that instruction is a necessary part of the task sequence. How can she report, then, that she's confused when the customary cue is omitted?
3. How can she tell us when she's bored or fearful?
4. How is this unconventional behavior working for this individual? Does it get her some attention? Does it make people leave her alone? Does it get her out of work? Does it get her some physical contact? Does she use it to initiate interactions? Does she use it to terminate interactions?

STRATEGIES

• Jack, a 19-year-old with autism, had just moved into a new supervised apartment. His parents had reported that he could dress himself independently, yet every morning staff would find him standing in front of his closet, seeming not to know what to do. By asking his family and themselves the question, "How might he be interpreting this?" they learned that Jack did in fact put his clothes on by himself, one item at a time, *after* one of his parents said, "Put your shirt on," "Put your socks on," "Put your pants on," and so forth. It seemed that Jack thought getting dressed meant having someone there to talk between each piece of clothing; that is, that the instruction was a necessary part of the task sequence. Staff decided to change as many things as they could about how and when Jack got dressed in the morning. Instead of having him get his clothes out in the morning and dress in his room, they had him pick his clothes out the night before and put them in the bathroom, where he would get dressed in the morning. With these changes in place, so that the activity appeared as different as possible to Jack, staff did not give him instructions for each step. Rather, they physically guided him through putting on each piece; after four mornings, Jack was able to dress himself independently.

- LaMere, a young woman having some emotional difficulties, spent at least half of her day in a resource class. Periodically in this class LaMere would throw all of her work around the room and begin screaming and crying about having too much to do. Typically the teacher then approached LaMere, asking her to calm down, and would suggest that they sit down to talk about what was upsetting her. LaMere seemed to enjoy these talks, but there never seemed to be anything in particular that was upsetting her. The teacher asked herself the question, "How might this behavior be working for LaMere?" She decided that it might be how LaMere was asking her for some individual time, just to talk. She began giving LaMere points for completing her assignments from her other classes, and told her that any time she had saved up 4 points she could ask for some time just to sit and talk. LaMere began completing her work and no longer needed to throw things and scream to get time alone to talk with her teacher.

- Joanne, a young woman with autism, lived in a small supervised apartment with two other women. Once or twice a month Joanne would begin pushing one of the other women with whom she lived. She would continue the pushing, gradually increasing the force of the push, until one of the staff came over and just held her still in a chair. After about 15 minutes of being restrained, Joanne would calm down and go about her business as usual. Staff asked the question, "How might this behavior be working for Joanne?" They hypothesized that she might be doing it to get physical contact from the staff. When they looked at her experiences across her days, they realized that the times she was restrained were the only times she received any kind of physical contact from another person. At one of their regular house meetings, everyone discussed affection and some ways of showing it. Staff and other residents began giving each other hugs when they retired for the day. Joanne's pushing decreased as she learned to accept and give hugs.

Conclusion

In deciding to intrude upon another person's being and change her behavior, we should examine the context within which the behavior is occurring. The context should be one in which the individual, regardless of level of impairment, has the opportunity to learn to live, work, and enjoy recreation in natural settings with their nonhandicapped peers and others.

Such a context is provided through a meaningful, chronological-age-appropriate, functional, community-based curriculum. When an unconventional behavior is seen as a problem, the context in which it occurs should be examined through a functional analysis. Staff can begin such an analysis by asking assessment questions about the ecology, curriculum, instruction, and, of course, possible communicative functions the behavior might be serving.

While we do not know that all behavior is an attempt by a learner to "tell" us something, we do know that all behavior has the potential to communicate important information. For example, even stereotypic behaviors, which may serve a relaxation or self-regulatory function, may tell us that the individual is anxious and upset in certain situations. In any "state-of-the-art" program, assessment of ecological, instructional, curricular, and communicative variables is an ongoing process that can help staff to develop strategies that preclude, prevent, and redirect even the most serious behavior problems.

POSITIVE PROGRAMMING STRATEGIES

In addition to change strategies that can be developed from a good functional assessment, we encourage staff to learn how to develop specific positive programming strategies. For clarity's sake we will define *positive programming* as a gradual educational process for behavior change that is based on a functional analysis of the presenting problems and involves systematic instruction in more effective ways of behaving.

Positive programming is actually the most important and useful of all the nonaversive interventions we present in this book. We make the distinction here between positive programming and other specific procedures for facilitating behavior change, which have an "on/off" quality. They are either in effect or they are not. Positive programming, as we are defining it, is a more consistent process that teaches new behavior over time and considers the behaviors required by learners to function in current and subsequent environments. This is in contrast to procedures for behavior change that focus on more discrete manipulations of specified undesirable behavior. Simply stated, we are discussing systematic, long-term skill building, rather than specific behavior reduction.

For example, if the target behavior of concern is "threatening others verbally," staff can reinforce the individual for not cursing. Another positive programming approach that could be used, instead or in addition, is an assertiveness or social skills training program that would provide the individual with a wider repertoire of alternative means of getting his way in a more acceptable manner. Reinforcing the individual for "not cursing" is a DRO procedure (see chapter 6). Teaching him other behavior by which to get his way is a positive programming strategy.

There are a number of examples of positive programming that are illustrative of this approach:

1. Teaching a new behavior or class of behaviors
2. Substituting communicative means
3. Teaching related but more appropriate alternative behaviors
4. Assigning meaning

But the range of options for positive programming is only limited by the imagination of the personnel working with the learner.

Teaching New Behavior

One of the key positive programming strategies is teaching a new behavior or class of behaviors. Several examples follow:

- Jane was depressed because she did not have any friends. When she was depressed she would sulk and not participate in various activities. Her school counselor taught her some strategies for meeting other students, and the speech and language therapist worked with her on her conversation skills. As she began to make new friends, she became less depressed and participated more frequently.
- Hazel was a 24-year-old woman challenged by the problem of autism. She lived in a small group home and attended a day activity center. Her daily tantrums often left hundreds of dollars worth of furniture in ruins. Her group home program shifted its focus to teaching functional, community-based skills such as shopping, ordering in a restaurant, bowling, and the like. Further, she was transferred to a supported work program in which she was rapidly placed in and trained to perform a competitive job at a local pizza parlor. As she gradually became more and more competent in performing these various chronological-age-appropriate skills in natural settings in which she had the opportunity to interact with nonhandicapped people, and as these activities took up more and more of her time, her tantrums gradually stopped occurring.
- Ted was out of school 2 or 3 days per week, either truant or ill. After a functional analysis, his counselor suspected that he was afraid to come to school because he had so many problems with other preadolescents on the school yard. She and Ted's teacher developed a social skills training

program for Ted that taught him to be more assertive and less frightened with his peers.

Communication Strategies

A second example of positive programming is teaching alternative communication strategies as substitutes for unconventional behaviors that serve a communicative function for the individual. The following examples serve as illustrations:

- Ellen was a 15-year-old in a class for adolescents labeled "behavior disordered." After reviewing the data on her outbursts in the lunchroom and around the building, her teacher determined that they occurred almost entirely on Friday and Monday, twice each month. He inquired of Ellen's friends and ascertained that there was "something wrong at home." The teacher and school psychologist met with Ellen and determined that she was in fact being abused when her uncle was at home from his job as a long-distance trucker. Although Ellen was a competent communicator under most situations, she did not know what to do or who to tell in this situation. Her problem behavior was for her a communication that she was very troubled. Once the authorities removed the uncle from her home and Ellen was assigned to a counselor she liked and trusted, she gradually learned how to talk about her problems rather than having outbursts. Eventually she learned how to be assertive outside of her sessions as well, when confronted with stressful situations.
- Matt had a problem with severe head banging. After a functional analysis, his residential support staff realized that the behavior occurred most often when a task was very challenging to Matt. They added to his picture communication board a sign asking for help and taught him to use it whenever a situation was very hard for him. When help was immediately given, the necessity for head banging was reduced.
- Joanne, a woman with retardation, was also legally deaf and blind. She had a fairly extensive sign vocabulary. Sometimes she was aggressive and self-abusive, behavior that appeared to serve multiple functions, such as asking for help, for a break, and for other interactions. Her vocational supervisor hypothesized that Joanne could not predict when her signs would "work" for her because she could not see or hear if someone was nearby and attending to her. Her supervisor gave her a desk bell similar to those used in hotel lobbies and taught her to ring it three times in a row to draw someone's attention before she signed. The bell as a communicative device, paired with the signs, eliminated her aggressive and self-injurious behavior.

- Mike screamed or had a tantrum any time he wanted something. He was beginning to speak but did not have many of the labels for things he wanted. His teacher in his early childhood program taught him to sign "want" and "help" while he was still learning to speak. As Mike increasingly used this new method of communication, he exhibited fewer and fewer tantrums.

Teaching More Appropriate Alternative Behaviors

With this strategy, positive programming consists of teaching more appropriate alternative behaviors to substitute for the unconventional or problematic behavior. It differs from the previous strategy in that the substitute behavior need not serve a communicative function. Both rely, of course, on a functional analysis of behavior. The following are examples:

- Jennie was a fidgety young woman who tended to pick at her skin when under stress. Her vocational counselor was concerned because this behavior resulted in unsightly sores that made it impossible for her to continue to work in a restaurant. As a substitute for the picking behavior, she taught Jennie to carry a tube of skin moisturizer cream. When Jennie was feeling stressed and thought she would begin to pick the skin on her arm and face, she learned to take out the cream and smooth it on other parts of her body (hands, lower arms, etc.). Most of the sores disappeared, and her skin became quite smooth and healthy looking.
- Beverly was an adult with profound handicaps. Her major activity, given a choice, was to drop items on the floor. Her vocational job coach decided to get her a job in the community library, where one of her co-workers sorted books that came into the repository and where Beverly's job was to put them in the appropriate bins. As a result, all day long she was able to drop items, which she liked, and receive subminimum wage for doing it.

Assigning Meaning

Sometimes behaviors can be shaped into communications by assigning meaning to them even when the intentionality is unclear, as in these examples:

- Rudy, a young man with autism, had no verbal means of communication and rarely initiated interactions. Periodically, throughout his day, he placed himself very close to his instructors. Staff began to respond to this proximity behavior as if it were an initiation for social interaction or a request for an object. Over time his movements became intentional and staff were able to begin shaping additional gestures.

- Emily frequently slapped her legs with considerable force. Sometimes it appeared to be when she wanted something that was out of her reach. Staff began responding to leg slaps as if she were asking for help, and would get her what they thought she wanted. Soon the slaps became more intentional, and, as Emily began to recognize that they would be responded to quickly, the intensity of the slaps decreased. After several weeks staff were able to get her to clap her hands when she needed help; eventually they were able to teach her to sign for help.

Conclusion

There are a number of advantages to using positive programming as a strategy for the reduction of behavior problems in the classroom and other settings. These advantages include

1. *Positive and constructive nature:* New behaviors are taught, minimizing the risk of the development of new problem behaviors.
2. *Long-term and lasting effects:* A new repertoire is built which can be maintained by the natural contingencies in the environment, providing a greater likelihood for generalizing such gains over time.
3. *Efficiency:* Positive programming uses whatever limited resources may be available in a given setting and reduces the behavior problem while contributing to general educational and developmental goals.
4. *Social validity:* The concerns and feelings of both the learner and others in her environment are addressed.
5. *Contribution to dignity:* This approach enables the learner to participate actively in the management of her own behavior and in making her own decisions.

Positive programming, as we have defined it, should be the primary approach in attempting to deal with any long-standing and serious problem behavior. It is only in the context of such a program that other procedures can be properly considered. If the effects of positive programming are not rapid enough or sufficient, however, it may be necessary to add one or more of the other intervention procedures discussed in the rest of the book. Note that we have said *add*, not *substitute*. A positive program should provide the base for the use of other strategies, such as reinforcement and shaping techniques, appropriate prompts and clearer instructions, and a variety of other positive behavior management procedures.

2

Basic Behavioral Technology

The purpose of this chapter is to provide a brief review and supply definitions for and examples of some of the widely used terms and procedures in the behavioral literature. If you require more in-depth information on basic behavioral principles and procedures, we would suggest any of the texts cited in the bibliography at the end of this book.

RESPONSE

A *response* (R) is defined as an *observable, measurable behavior. Observable* refers to being able to be seen, as opposed to inferred. Thus, for these discussions a response is considered behavior that can be seen. For a response to be *measurable* it must be describable in terms of specific and clear criteria. Defining a response in these terms initially appears to be relatively simple; however, this misconception often results in serious errors and difficulties in behavior change programs. Consider, for example, the definition of the response "raising one's hand." Most of us would consider that phrase alone to be a simple and clear enough definition of the response. There are several questions, however, that are left unanswered. If someone were to measure that response, based on that definition, which of the examples in Figure 2.1 would be included? The figure provides a good illustration of why definitions of responses must be such that two or more people could observe and describe the same thing. Good response definitions tell what the response looks like on every critical dimension. In the case of hand raising, critical dimensions might be how high the hand is raised or how long it is held up.

Defining responses in an observable and measurable manner is critical for at least the following reasons:

1. It increases the effectiveness of behavior change procedures.
2. It improves support staff's ability to be consistent in their reaction to a certain response.

FIGURE 2.1.   Some variations on hand raising

3. It facilitates detection of contingencies for the learner.
4. It increases the possibility of consistency across support staff.
5. It allows for measurement of effectiveness of various instructional strategies, training programs, behavior change programs, and so forth.

CONSEQUENCE

A *consequence* (C) is defined as an environmental stimulus or event that contingently follows the occurrence of a particular response and, as a result of that contingency relationship, strengthens or weakens the future occurrence of that response. Some consequences that might appear in the everyday job or classroom setting include:

Extra break time
Praise from trainer or coach
Bonus pay
Being able to leave early
A day off
Tokens
Going to lunch with a co-worker

Remember, in determining a consequence it is critical to state (1) the contingency rule that relates it to the response (i.e., what specific observable and measurable response must occur in order for a specific consequence to occur) and (2) the effect the consequence is likely to have on the future occurrence of the response. For example, teacher attention is considered a consequence if it is given contingently, upon the occurrence of certain behavior (e.g., signing for help). Data collection will show if the contingent attention serves to increase or decrease future "help" responses.

Different kinds of consequences and different kinds of contingency relationships between response and consequences can have very different effects on future occurrences of the response. The various kinds of consequences and contingency relationships will be discussed throughout the remainder of this book. Here we will focus on the basic consequences and contingency relationships as represented by the event matrix shown in Figure 2.2.

Positive Reinforcement

Positive reinforcement occurs when the contingent *presentation* of a certain stimulus or stimulus event results in a *future increase* or strengthening, over time, of response rate, duration, or intensity. A reinforcer can only be determined by the effect it has on the response over time, not by a single event.

Remember, the word *reinforcement* in this term refers to the increasing or strengthening of a response over time. The word *positive* refers to the presentation or addition of a particular stimulus or event, *not* to the nature of the stimulus or event (i.e., whether it is pleasant or unpleasant).

FIGURE 2.2.
Event matrix for applications of reinforcement and punishment

	Contingent presentation of stimulus	Contingent removal of stimulus	Withholding of previous consequence
Increase in response rate	Positive reinforcement	Negative reinforcement	Recovery after punishment
Decrease in response rate	Punishment I	Punishment II	Extinction

When using positive reinforcement, keep in mind these important characteristics:

1. It increases behavior, whether you want it to or not (e.g., negative attention can increase unwanted behavior).
2. It must be presented contingently.
3. It must be presented immediately and consistently.
4. It can be primary or unlearned, such as food, physical contact, or drink.
5. It can be secondary or conditioned, such as with a token or point system, which may be traded for a primary reinforcer.
6. It needs to be individualized for person, time, and place, and should be as age-appropriate and nonstigmatizing as possible.
7. It can lose effectiveness if too much is used.
8. It can be social (attention from someone, time to spend with someone, a chance to talk to a friend).
9. It can be the opportunity to engage in a preferred activity.

Following are some examples of positive reinforcement:

- Zachary received a token for every math problem he solved correctly. Over time, the correct number increased.
- Every time Sebrina talked out, her supervisor went to her and asked her to keep her comments to herself. Over time, Sebrina talked out more and more.
- Each time Kathy remembered to bring her bus ticket, she received praise from her teacher and boarded the city bus by herself. Now Kathy rarely forgets her bus ticket.
- Every time Sandy made a mistake she cried and someone consoled her. Soon Sandy made more and more mistakes.

DETERMINING REINFORCERS

Determining reinforcers is a critical component in any teaching or behavior change program. Again, the only reliable way to determine if a consequence is a reinforcer is by examining whether or not the response increases in rate, duration, or magnitude over time. The following are some ways to determine which consequences are at least potential reinforcers for a learner:

1. Ask the learner what he likes.
2. Ask the learner what he would be willing to work for.

3. Ask familiar others what the individual has been willing to work for in the past.
4. Observe the learner, to determine how he spends his free time.
5. Review records to learn what has operated as a reinforcer in the past.
6. Offer the learner a variety of things and activities and record what he most frequently chooses.

An ecological assessment should be carried out to determine what reinforcers are naturally or typically available in the situation in which learning is to occur. Using these reinforcers, where possible, increases the likelihood that the behavior will be naturally maintained after the support staff fades out.

SCHEDULES OF REINFORCEMENT: CONTINUOUS AND INTERMITTENT

Schedules of reinforcement have predictable effects on the characteristics of the response. These are discussed in several of the basic texts listed in the bibliography. The schedule is the predetermined rule by which reinforcement is delivered or withheld for a given behavior.

Continuous reinforcement (CRF) involves a schedule in which reinforcement is delivered following *every* occurrence of the targeted response. While it is true that many behaviors are learned through reinforcement that is delayed or intermittent, such learning is often slower and less efficient. Generally, new behaviors will be learned more rapidly if they are reinforced every time they occur. Consider the following example:

- Meg was crying. As a more conventional means for initiating an interaction she was taught to sign for what she needed. Initially, every time Meg used the designated appropriate sign, she received an appropriate reaction immediately.

Timing of the delivery of reinforcement is critical, especially when attempting to teach a *new* response. Behavior that produces an immediate consequence will be more strongly affected by the reinforcer than when the consequence is delayed. Once a behavior or skill has been established through the use of a continuous schedule, it may be considered "weak," because if the reinforcement is stopped it is likely that the response will quickly cease. Additionally, there are many situations in which maintaining such a consequence schedule would be difficult or impossible.

Once a response is established, therefore, it is necessary to change systematically to an intermittent schedule of reinforcement, which is more likely to maintain and strengthen the behavior of concern. With *intermit-*

tent reinforcement some but not all occurrences of a behavior are reinforced. There are four basic intermittent schedules that are most relevant
to instructional situations: fixed ratio, variable ratio, fixed interval, and
variable interval. The most useful in terms of fading from a continuous to
an intermittent schedule are ratio schedules.

Fixed-Ratio Schedule. A fixed-ratio (FR) schedule of reinforcement
is one in which a reinforcer is given upon completion of a given number of
responses, such as after every 5 responses, after every 10 responses, after
every 60 responses, and so forth. Consider the following example:

- The job coach has set up Debbie's work station, requiring her to
  assemble and collate 25 packets of materials in order to receive a 10-
  minute break. Debbie does not receive a break until she has completed 25 packets. Figure 2.3 shows how this might look on a given
  day.

The FR schedule produces a response pattern that is similar, regardless
of the ratio size. Once the first response has been made, the remaining
responses are completed rapidly with minimal hesitation between responses. After reinforcement, there is a characteristic pause (called a *post-
reinforcement pause*) before the next set of responses is initiated. The
length of this pause is related to the size of the ratio. If the ratio is large, the
pause will be long. If the ratio is small, the pause will likely be short. If the
ratio is very small, the pause may be so brief that it is difficult to detect.
This feature is a critical one to keep in mind, as can be seen in the following example:

- Dean worked at a plant assembling basic switches to be used in
  airplanes. When the job was first set up, Dean was required to
  assemble 10 switches, after which he received a check on his production card from his job trainer and was immediately directed to
  assemble another 10 switches. After assembling 30 to 40 switches,
  Dean would leave the work area and refuse to return. The job
  trainer began allowing Dean a 1- to 2-minute break between sets of
  10 switches. Soon Dean was able to assemble as many as 100
  switches a day.

FIGURE 2.3.   Fixed-ratio schedule of reinforcement for Debbie's work

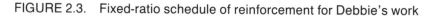
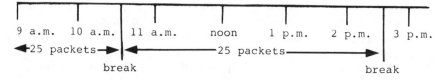

Variable-Ratio Schedule. A variable-ratio (VR) schedule of reinforcement is one in which reinforcement is delivered after a variable number of responses are made; however, this number is a specified average. It may be decided, for example, that, on the *average*, every 15 responses will be reinforced. Thus the VR schedule is a function of the number of responses made, as in the following case:

- The reinforcement schedule developed to meet one of Lisa's primary activities this year has been arranged in a variable-ratio format. When, on the average across a day, she initiated three conversations of at least 2 minutes each with her classmates, she received an exchangeable token for her behavior. The criterion for reinforcement was predetermined each time (e.g., reinforcement delivered after three, five, two, four, or one 2-minute conversations); but, over time, the average was three.

One of the best-known examples of the VR schedule is a slot machine. Clearly, this kind of schedule produces very strong and consistent response rates. Because reinforcement on a VR schedule is less predictable, it typically produces more consistent rates of responding.

The VR schedule is important for the type of response rates it produces and also because it is a kind of reinforcement schedule that occurs often in everyday life. Examples of "typical" behaviors that are maintained by VR schedules are selling door-to-door, playing the lottery, and playing cards.

Fixed-Interval Schedule. A fixed-interval (FI) reinforcement schedule is one in which reinforcement opportunity occurs after a specified or fixed interval of time, measured from the preceding reinforcement. If the time interval is 2 minutes, the schedule is called an *FI 2-minute schedule.* Regardless of the length of the interval, on an FI schedule, the first response to occur after the interval is completed yields reinforcement, as in the following example:

- For Larry, picking up his paycheck each week on Friday is a very reinforcing event. Consequently, *every* Friday at 4:00 P.M., Larry picks up his check at the central office immediately following his work week. If he goes before the interval is up (e.g., on Thursday), his check will not be available.

This type of schedule produces a predictable response pattern where responses gradually increase as time goes by, until the end of the interval, where a very high rate of responding is seen. This pattern is referred to as a *fixed-interval scallop.* Such a situation is typically seen in any situation where a deadline is involved, as in the following:

- John had to write three stories during the 9-week semester. One story was due every 3 weeks, after which his mom took him out for a special pizza dinner (an FI 3-week schedule). John's rate of working on the story increased gradually as the deadline approached, with the most intense amount of work occurring the last two nights before each story was due.

Variable-Interval Schedule.   A variable-interval (VI) schedule of reinforcement is one in which reinforcement becomes available after the passage of varying intervals of time around some specified average, such as after an average of 5 minutes has elapsed. Note that, under a VI schedule, reinforcement may become *available* after a given period of time, but it is not *delivered* until the required response is made. As with the FI schedule, this type of schedule is time dependent. The passage of time alone, however, does not bring about the reinforcement; only the correct response *after* the interval has expired will bring about reinforcement, as seen in the following example:

- Kevin works in a laundry, sorting wash and loading machines. He earns extra social time with his job coach for staying on task. On the *average* of every 20 minutes his coach checks to see if Kevin is working. If he is, he receives a plus on his supervision sheet. Each plus earns him an extra 2 minutes of social time at the end of the day.

As with the other schedules of reinforcement that have been discussed, the VI schedule also produces a typical response pattern. Generally, the smaller the average interval between opportunities for reinforcement, the higher the rate of responding will be. Thus, the frequency of availability of reinforcement in various environments is a critical feature to examine. Expecting high rates of appropriate behavior in barren environments with few support staff available is unrealistic.

The most important aspect of the VI schedule is that, once the proper average interval has been determined, such a schedule generates and maintains a consistent response rate, as exemplified by the persistent fishing enthusiast. This may be particularly important in certain job sites, as the VI schedule encourages consistently hard but not necessarily fast work.

Implementation Issues.   Increases in ratios or intervals in these schedules should be made gradually. If increases are made too quickly or are too large, the response may not be maintained and in fact may decrease.

Some researchers have suggested that the interval schedules can be strengthened by limiting access to the reinforcer, once it becomes available. So, for example, if the reinforcer becomes available after a 5-minute interval is up, the schedule would be strengthened if the reinforcer were then only available for 2 minutes. Thus, if the response does not occur soon after the interval begins, it is not reinforced, as the following case illustrates:

- Mike, a teacher in a resource room for students with behavioral disabilities, was interested in helping his students stay on task more. He set up a variable-interval schedule where the average interval length was 10 minutes. So, on the average of every 10 minutes, he would walk around the classroom. If students were working, they received a small check on their "on task" card. For every two checks they earned an extra minute of free time at the end of the period, but checks were only available for as long as it took Mike to walk around the classroom.

Sometimes staff are concerned that, just as they are about to deliver a reinforcer, the learner does something inappropriate. Naturally, they do not want to reinforce such a behavior. In this case, it is wise to think about a brief delay before making the reinforcer available. This is known as *limited hold*:

- Matthew works at a restaurant putting glasses in the dishwasher. On the *average* of every 10 minutes his job coach checks to see if Matthew is putting in the glasses. As the coach approached to deliver the token, Matthew shouted at another student. The job coach decided to wait 1 minute before delivering the reinforcer, so as not to reinforce Matthew inadvertently for shouting.

Negative Reinforcement

When the contingent *removal* of a certain stimulus or event results in a *future increase* or strengthening, over time, of response rate, duration, or intensity, negative reinforcement has occurred. The word *negative* in this term indicates that a stimulus or event has been contingently *removed* or *taken away*. It does *not* mean the consequence itself is negative. The following are some examples of negative reinforcement:

- It was chilly in the room. Don closed the window. The chill was "taken away," and from now on when it is chilly Don immediately closes any open window.
- It was very noisy in the gym. Cheryl covered her ears and cried. The classroom aide let her leave. In the future when Cheryl is in the gym and it is noisy, she will be likely again to cover her ears and cry.
- Mr. Murphy habitually told his class to quiet down. Every time they yelled, he told them to stop and for a few minutes they did, but soon began again. He repeatedly told them to stop, and now con-

tinues to do so each time they yell. Mr. Murphy's behavior has been negatively reinforced.

- Frank was in a small group where the objective was to increase students' communicative skills. Frank thought it was boring and began to engage in abusive language. He was removed from the group by the staff. Frank's language continues to be abusive when it is time for group.

Because negative reinforcement depends upon the presence of unpleasant or aversive conditions, the procedure has limited usefulness for instructional situations. Nonetheless, it is important to understand it for at least the following reasons:

1. It can strengthen both appropriate and inappropriate behavior.
2. It is used as often by learners to change the behavior of staff as the reverse.
3. It is *not* punishment.
4. Awareness of the concept is useful in helping individuals learn to express that certain things that are naturally occurring or are not under their control are unpleasant. In one of the examples just given, the noisy gym provides a natural opportunity for teaching Cheryl to express that she is uncomfortable and to say/sign/touch a picture indicating that she wants to leave.

Punishment

Unlike negative reinforcement, which *increases* behavior, punishment *decreases* behavior. There are basically two types of punishment.

TYPE I PUNISHMENT

Type I punishment refers to the contingent *presentation* of a stimulus or event which results in a *future decrease* or weakening of response rate, duration, or intensity. These consequences may include:

1. Naturally occurring results of various behaviors, such as getting sick after eating too much junk food or getting cold hands when mittens are taken off in the snow
2. Events that are arranged by others, such as a spanking, having to "overclean" a room, or being squirted in the mouth with Tabasco sauce

The following examples are fairly typical:

- Monica played with the knickknacks on her mother's table. Each time she did, her mother said, "No," and slapped Monica's hand. Now Monica does not touch the things on her mother's table, at least when her mom is around.
- Jeremy pushed over a chair in class. His teacher made him fix it (restitution), then made him move and clean all the other chairs in the room (overcorrection). Now the frequency of Jeremy pushing over chairs is lessened.

TYPE II PUNISHMENT

Type II punishment refers to the contingent *withdrawal* of a stimulus or event which results in a *future decrease* or weakening of response rate, duration, or intensity. This type of punishment includes consequences that fall into the categories of time out from positive reinforcement and response cost. These are some examples:

- Mark grabbed materials from other children. The vocational instructor put him in a time-out chair. Over time, the grabbing decreased, as did Mark's interactions with his peers.
- Mike put game pieces in his mouth. His mother took the game away (response cost). Over time, Mike quit putting the game pieces in his mouth and also quit playing the game with his mother.
- Emily bit her fingers while she was working. Every time she did so, her job trainer took points away (response cost). She reduced the amount of time she bit her fingers and began to refuse assistance from her job coach.

PROBLEMS WITH USING PUNISHMENT

There is a host of problems in using even mild punishment of either type I or II:

1. It can produce social withdrawal (punishee avoids punisher).
2. It can produce aggression (punishee may aggress against punisher or third party).
3. It can produce emotional side effects (shyness, unresponsiveness, etc.).
4. It can become "addictive" to the punisher, particularly because it often has immediate though short-term effects.

5. It does not eliminate behavior, but only suppresses it, especially if an alternative or replacement behavior is not taught.
6. It does not build replacement behaviors.
7. It is often only temporary. When punishment is stopped, the behavior is likely to return, perhaps in worse form than before punishment began.
8. It can inhibit behaviors other than those being intentionally punished.
9. It can be very situation- and person-specific in its effects.

Remember, reinforcers and punishers are determined by how they affect behavior. Because a learner appears to like or dislike something (or because we think he should) does not necessarily make it a reinforcer or a punisher. When punishment is stopped, behavior typically returns to its previous strength. This is known as *recovery after punishment* (refer to Figure 2.2, above) and is similar to the effects of stopping reinforcement — known as *extinction* — but with the reverse effect.

Extinction

Another procedure shown in the event matrix of Figure 2.2 is extinction. This is another procedure for decreasing behavior, one that shares several of the same side effects and disadvantages as punishment procedures.

Extinction is the withholding of a previously available consequence (the discontinuation of a contingency relationship between a response and a consequence) which results in a decrease or weakening of response rate, duration, or intensity. In other words, a behavior which, under certain conditions was followed by a reinforcing consequence, is no longer followed by that consequence and decreases under those conditions. Here are two examples:

- Joe told jokes in workshop, and all the other students laughed. The teacher instructed them to ignore Joe's jokes except at recess. They did and soon Joe quit telling jokes in class.
- Staci received praise from her husband each time she fixed a gourmet meal. She began fixing more, and he began to expect them, no longer giving her praise. Soon she went back to fixing quick-and-easy (though boring) meals.

There are certain characteristics about extinction that need to be kept in mind:

1. Extinction is often hard to apply because of the difficulty in identifying and controlling the consequences maintaining a response. This is particularly true for a behavior that has been present for a long period of time and consequently has had a variety of reinforcing conditions available. Additionally, it is not unusual for specific behavior patterns to be maintained by multiple sources of reinforcement.

2. In using an extinction procedure, there may be an initial increase in the behavior that is no longer being reinforced. Joe, the joke teller, for example, may initially think that his fellow students stopped laughing because his jokes weren't funny enough. He may, therefore, decide to try to tell funnier jokes. This factor takes on greater importance if the behaviors involved are potentially dangerous. For example, one would not want to use an extinction procedure with a child who runs away or with a worker who shouts out on the job because an escalation of these behaviors could have serious consequences.

3. Extinction only works if the identified reinforcement maintaining the undesired behavior can be completely controlled. Obviously this presents difficulties across a variety of environments.

4. Some side effects such as aggression and emotional problems may occur, especially when very valuable and meaningful consequences (such as attention from others) are no longer forthcoming. This is especially true if the learner is not taught alternative or replacement behaviors for achieving the same end.

5. Extinction procedures may have to be continued over long periods of time.

6. An extinction procedure typically results in a slow decline in the non-reinforced behavior. Therefore, extinction should be used with caution if the need is for an immediate and rapid decline.

7. The number of times a given behavior pattern or response will occur after an extinction procedure is begun depends upon the following:
    a. The number of times the behavior has been reinforced prior to the beginning of the extinction procedure
    b. The type and magnitude of previous reinforcing experiences
    c. The pattern or schedule of reinforcement previously provided
    d. The availability of alternative means of behaving that will produce the same or equally valuable reinforcers.

8. Behaviors that are being maintained by a continuous schedule of reinforcement are typically easier to extinguish than those on an intermittent schedule.

9. Behaviors on variable rather than fixed schedules are more resistant to extinction.

10. If replacement behaviors are not taught, other problematic or uncon-

ventional behaviors may replace those that have been put under extinction.

11. More than the target behavior may be eliminated by an extinction procedure.

12. Extinction works best when competing and/or replacement behaviors are systematically and simultaneously reinforced. (See comments about the 100% rule in chapter 8, on Differential Reinforcement of Alternative Behaviors.)

DISCRIMINATIVE STIMULUS

The final item in this chapter's discussion of basic behavioral technology is the discriminative stimulus (S^D). This is an environmental stimulus, cue, or event that sets the occasion for a particular response by indicating the availability of a particular result or consequence. An S^D lets us and our learners know when a certain behavior has the potential for a certain result, as in the following examples:

- For many groups of students, the presence of a substitute teacher is the discriminative stimulus that sets the occasion for more talking out than usual. In her presence they receive more attention for talking out than with their regular teacher.
- In a department store, the clerk is the discriminative stimulus that sets the occasion for requesting help, since his presence indicates that help is now available if it is requested.

A discriminative stimulus can be either a naturally occurring event (a sunny day setting the occasion for a picnic) or one that has been arranged (an invitation indicating the availability of a party). The important point to remember is that the S^D merely indicates the availability of a certain result, but it does not independently bring about the response.

The contingency relationship between the discriminative stimulus, response, and the consequence can be stated as follows: If a particular response occurs in the presence of or immediately following the presentation of a stimulus, it will result in a particular consequence in accordance with some schedule. This basic contingency relationship underlies both the instructional and the behavior change techniques that are described in later chapters of this book.

3

Instructional Technology

Most individuals are able to learn through natural, fairly casual presentation of materials and experiences. As long as they have sufficient opportunity to practice, they eventually "get it." For many learners with severe communication disorders, including those with autism, social/behavioral disorders, and other severe cognitive handicaps, the world is often difficult to sort out and learning is a struggle. These learners present a special challenge to teachers and staff. Fortunately, technology is available that is very helpful in teaching these learners.

This chapter will first present how learning takes place for cognitively normal learners and then discuss some of the technology for learners with severe communication and cognitive disorders, specifically, the modified discrete-trial format, shaping, and chaining.

COGNITIVELY NORMAL LEARNERS

Before explaining the technology for learners with special needs, we will show how learning usually occurs for those who do not have cognitive handicaps. This will help us to understand where learners with communication disorders may be experiencing difficulties.

Basic Learning Paradigm

Consider the diagram of a basic learning paradigm shown in Figure 3.1. This represents how learning typically occurs. In this paradigm, stimuli and instruction occur naturally and eventually increase the learner's ability to sort out cues, responses, and consequences. To help visualize how this format works in practice, we will go through it step by step, using the task of learning to answer the telephone as our example.

The first step (labeled 1 in the diagram) is the perception of a natural

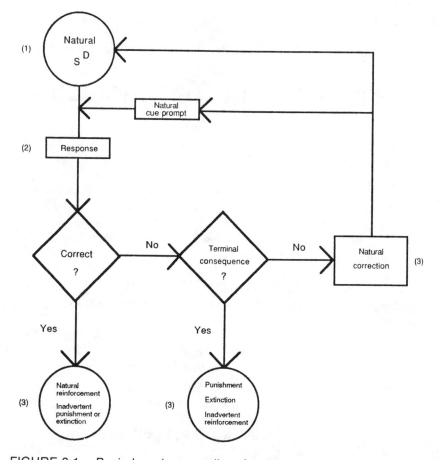

FIGURE 3.1.   Basic learning paradigm for the typical learning process in a natural setting

stimulus or cue (S^D), in this case, the telephone ringing. Sometimes the natural cue includes a prompt such as when the phone rings repeatedly, thus presenting the stimulus over and over.

The second step (labeled 2) is the response to the S^D, in this case, answering the telephone. The obvious question is, Was the response correct? The correctness of the response leads to the third step, the consequence, which in this paradigm could be any of those items labeled 3. The following are the possibilities:

1. If the response is correct, there are two possibilities:
   a. We receive natural reinforcement (one of our friends is on the phone).
   b. We are put on inadvertent extinction or are punished (there is no one on the line or it is a wrong number).
2. If the response is incorrect because we do not answer the phone quickly enough there are three possibilities:
   a. We are punished by the sound of the dial tone.
   b. We are put on extinction (there is no one on the line).
   c. We are inadvertently reinforced (we pick up the phone, and although we missed the first call, there just happens to be someone else calling).
3. Also, it is possible that if the response is incorrect we may receive a natural correction (the person calls back) and we get another chance to respond.

Contrived Teaching Paradigm

The learning paradigm just described works so well for most of us that teachers have taken it into the classroom and attempted to use it there. In the classroom, however, there are fewer natural cues, so the result is what we have called a "contrived" teaching paradigm (see Figure 3.2).

Note that the parts of the process are nearly identical to the basic learning paradigm. However, because the natural environment may not provide learners with sufficient opportunity for practice or provide enough information for skills to be learned easily or quickly, teachers sometimes must also use artificial stimuli, prompts, corrections, and materials.

Following the steps in Figure 3.2, consider how a teacher might present a lesson to students who are learning about safety issues regarding telephone use. First, at step 1, because they are at school, a special (or artificial) S^D must be used. A limited-line telephone rings, a student answers it, and a pretend male "stranger" asks if Joan is there, saying that Joan is his sister. At step 2, there is a response: The student answers yes or no. Depending upon the correctness of the response, one of several consequences occurs (step 3):

1. For a correct response ("Yes, but she can't come to the phone"), the teacher may provide artificial reinforcement (praise or perhaps some special reward).
2. For an incorrect response ("No, she's not here"), the teacher may not reinforce the answer or may reprimand the learner.

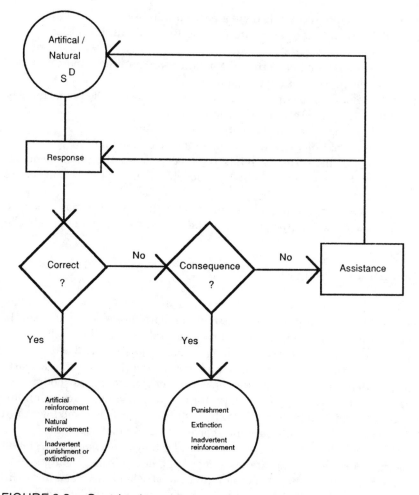

FIGURE 3.2.   Contrived teaching paradigm

3. Or, if the response is incorrect, the teacher may provide some assistance
   to the learner, for example, by telling him what he should have said,
   and asking him to try again.

   Consider the typical learner's point of view when learning occurs under
this contrived paradigm, as depicted in Figure 3.3. Each step is shown
in terms of the subjective, internal processes of the cognitively normal
learner.

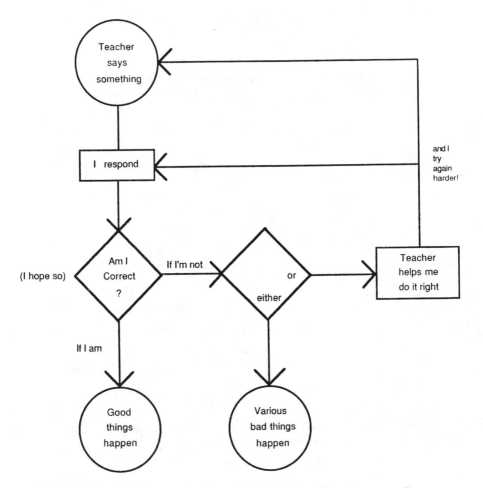

FIGURE 3.3.   The learner's view of the contrived teaching paradigm

THE COGNITIVELY/COMMUNICATIVELY DISORDERED LEARNER

While the basic and contrived paradigms work quite well for most learn-ers, this is not the case for the learner who has a more difficult time making sense of the world. A learner with autism or similar communication disor-der, for example, has a particularly difficult time making sense of verbal or social feedback. The same paradigm from her point of view probably looks like the diagram in Figure 3.4. As you can see, our typical contrived teaching paradigm may do little to help sort out the world for the person

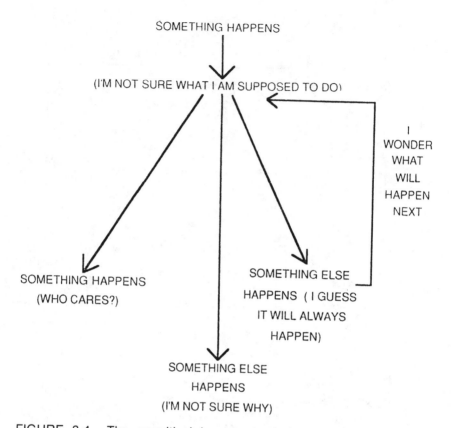

FIGURE 3.4. The cognitively/communicatively disordered learner's perspective on the contrived teaching paradigm

with severe learning problems. It remains a confusing and unpredictable place.

The discrete-trial format can be revised to present stimuli and instruction in a very specific and discrete way designed to increase the learner's ability to sort out cues, responses, and consequences. It may be viewed as shown in Figure 3.5. You will note two basic yet very critical differences between this discrete-trial format and the models presented earlier. First, the need for assistance to insure a correct response is assessed *before* the response occurs. Thus, if assistance is required, it is given before there is a chance for an incorrect response to occur. If assistance is not requested, it is not given at all during that particular trial. If an error is made, we complete that trial before we start another. Then we put the prompt in, wheth-

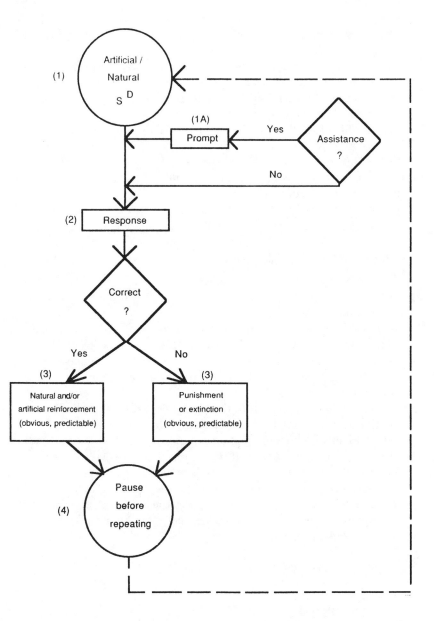

FIGURE 3.5.   Discrete-trial format for learners with cognitive/communi-cative disorders

er requested or not, before the error can occur. (The importance of the placement of assistance will be discussed further in chapter 4.)

The second basic difference is the addition of step 4 in the diagram — a pause at the end of the trial. The purpose of this pause is to give the message clearly that this particular trial is over and, in most cases, the next trial will be forthcoming. Separating the trials facilitates the learner's understanding of what goes into each trial. Without this pause the learner is likely to perceive a stream of events, few of which he can sort out.

Figure 3.6 shows how this modified format is perceived by the student with severe cognitive/communicative impairments, thus helping him to understand what is going to happen.

When using the discrete-trial format, it is important to remember the following points regarding each of the critical components:

INSTRUCTION/CUE/STIMULUS

1. It must be clear. It should not be able to be confused with or by any other stimulus.
2. It should be consistent. If the cue you choose to use is, "Put the laundry here," use essentially the same cue each time. Do not switch and use, "Fill the washer," unless you are sure your learner perceives it as the same cue. If you are not sure, do not take the risk of confusing the situation.
3. The cue should be relevant to the task or situation, and based upon the comprehension abilities of the learner.
4. It should only be presented when you are sure the learner is attending.
5. It should approximate the natural or terminal cue. This is particularly important when the task is one that should be performed independently. If the terminal cue for doing laundry is a pile of dirty clothes (you see the laundry and you do it), do not teach the learner to do laundry only in response to your verbal cue; rather, help him learn to do the laundry when he sees the dirty clothes are in a sizable pile.

PROMPTS

1. Be sure the prompt produces the correct response.
2. Be sure the prompt you use can be faded. For many learners with problems such as autism it is difficult to fade verbal prompts. Motor or spatial prompts may help. (More about prompts can be found in chapter 4.)

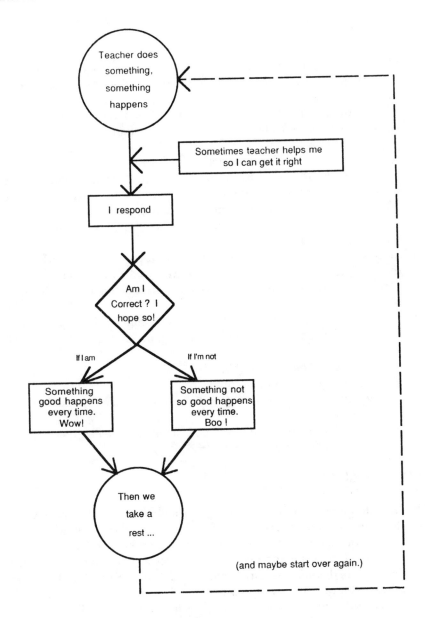

FIGURE 3.6. The cognitively/communicatively disordered learner's perspective on the discrete-trial format

RESPONSE

1. Make sure the response is defined in such a way that everyone can observe and describe the same response (see the discussion in chapter 2 on defining behavior).
2. Be sure the learner responds in a correct manner following the cue. Alternatively, have a plan for systematically chaining or shaping the response into the full task. For example, when beginning to teach table setting, the cue may be the stack of dishes on the table. The initial target response may be putting the plates out. Through chaining, the target response would be systematically expanded into setting the entire table. Without a systematic plan for changing the response, it is difficult to predict what response the learner may finally emit, and it may not be what you want.
3. Make sure you require only one response unit per cue; that is, don't up the ante. Accept whatever it is you have asked the learner to do, as shown in Figure 3.7, where the response unit is defined as folding four pieces of laundry.
4. Be sure to define what units of behavior comprise the response you want. The desired response can be one or more units of behavior, such as

> Folding one piece of clothing
> Folding five pieces of clothing
> Folding five pieces of clothing and putting each in the laundry basket
> Emptying the dryer, folding, and sorting all the clothing into appropriate baskets

CONSEQUENCE

1. As with the response, the consequence should be defined in such a way that everyone can observe it and describe the exact same thing.
2. Be sure the consequence you choose is demonstrably reinforcing. It is not enough to assume that the learner likes a particular consequence and that it therefore will be reinforcing. You can be sure the consequence you've chosen is a reinforcer only if, in using it, it actually increases the future occurrence of the behavior it follows.
3. Choose a consequence for an *incorrect response* which is clearly different from the consequence for a *correct response*. Obviously, a consequence for an incorrect response should not have reinforcing qualities and should communicate to the learner that the response was, in fact, not correct.

FIGURE 3.7.   The teacher should require only one response unit per cue and not ask for more

4. Choose a reinforcer that offers the best chance of being faded to the reinforcers available for that behavior in the natural environment. For example, in the natural environment, the reinforcer for saying, "I want a hamburger, please," is the server saying, "That'll be one burger," not the program staff saying, "That's good ordering, Mike."

When designing reinforcers so they can be faded to natural reinforcement, consider the following:

1. The level or magnitude of the reinforcer. For example:
   - A student earns time to spend with the principal. Initially, for this to be a reinforcing event, she gets to spend 20 minutes with him. A principal would not usually be able to spend that much time with one student every day, nor would a work supervisor in a subsequent environment. Fading the magnitude to a more natural level (e.g., one 10-minute meeting per week) would be an important goal.
   - A teacher working with a student on verbal requests uses popcorn as a reinforcer and gives out four or five pieces per request. In the natural environment such a request typically yields at least a handful and often a whole bag.

- A staff member gives out one sip of soft drink at a time for the learner performing his work. A more natural level is to receive a glass or even an entire can of the drink, which can happen at break time.
- A learner earns pennies in a token system. The vocational instructor charges her 5 cents for a candy bar. In the natural environment, it will cost at least 50 cents. The vocational instructor must consider this and make necessary changes in the system.

2. The kind of reinforcer. For example:
   - Bingo chips are seldom used as reinforcers in the natural environment. Begin with real money in any token system so that the only fade required will be with respect to amount.
3. The frequency of availability and delivery. For example:
   - One staff member convinced her principal to put a soda machine in her classroom so her students could practice using it and she could use it as a reinforcer. It was available to them after every activity (approximately 12 times per day, though they were only allowed to drink part of the sodas they bought). In other environments, students are not likely to have that kind of access to either the money or the soda machine.
4. The topography (physical characteristics) of the reinforcer. For example:
   - Physical therapists often give tickles as reinforcers. In many environments (particularly with older learners), a more appropriate form of reinforcer would be a pat on the back or a handshake.
   - Instead of hugs (except as periodic and genuine expressions of affection), use a handshake as a reinforcer.

INTERTRIAL INTERVAL

1. Remember to pause between each instructional unit.
2. Base the length of these pauses on the needs of the individual learner and the natural interval, when possible. A learner with a very short attention span may require very short intertrial intervals. The intertrial interval for many tasks in the natural environment is rarely just minutes long. An example is paying for food at the checkout. The natural intervals here vary in length, depending on how quickly one uses up the food and has to return for more.
3. Use the intertrial interval for natural conversation/interaction and for incidental teaching. For example, although during the trials you may be working specifically on assembly, you may take the time during the intertrial interval to talk about counting the parts being assembled.

4. Use this interval to record data and anecdotal notes on the previous trial, if the situation lends itself to note taking.

SHAPING

There are times when a response may not be in the exact form necessary to consider it correct. When this is the case it may be helpful to use a shaping procedure to establish the desired response. Shaping is a technique that can be used within the discrete-trial format or separately, depending on the individual task and learner.

Shaping involves reinforcing those variations or forms of a behavior that more or most closely approximate the target response, with the process being continued until the desired response is established. Shaping is also referred to as the method of *successive approximations*. An example of shaping is depicted in Figure 3.8, where the teacher offers reinforcement for successively longer periods of attention to a project, until the desired length of attention is achieved.

In addition to teaching new behavior, shaping can be used as a procedure for gradually modifying undesired behaviors that are already present.

FIGURE 3.8.   Shaping length of attention to a project

The same principle is employed: Begin with the current behavior and differentially reinforce successive approximations toward a more desirable and appropriate criterion. For example, a teacher may wish to reduce the frequency of tantrum behavior. Through the procedure of shaping, she will reinforce increasingly shorter, less intense, and less violent temper tantrums. When their intensity becomes more manageable, she will begin to shape increasingly more socially appropriate ways for her student to express his frustration and anger.

Technically, shaping means waiting for an occurrence of the variation of the behavior which is most similar to the desired behavior, and then reinforcing it. In practice, however, shaping can be used in combination with prompting, eliminating the need to wait for the approximation to occur.

Shaping also can be combined with the use of discriminative stimuli (S^Ds) to help set the occasion for the approximation of a particular response to occur. Thus, if a teacher is trying to shape "quiet working" in her class, she may raise a sign at particular times indicating that during that time students may earn points for working more quietly than usual.

Shaping can be combined with imitative prompting, whereby the approximation is demonstrated to the student by a teacher or other model. For example, a teacher might use imitative prompting to help a student learn to wait in the lunch line for increasingly longer periods of time.

To maintain a behavior that has been recently shaped, an appropriate reinforcement schedule must be implemented (see chapter 2).

To be most effective when using shaping,

1. Keep your terminal (ultimate) goal in mind.
2. Begin with behaviors in the individual's repertoire.
3. Begin with behaviors that most closely resemble the individual's goal.
4. Select a step size that can be easily, but not too easily, achieved.
5. Remain at a given step long enough for the individual to incorporate it firmly into his repertoire, but no longer.
6. Watch for behavioral disintegration; if it appears to be occurring, drop back a step or two.
7. Use effective reinforcement procedures throughout.

The desired behavior must be clearly defined to include all the possible response dimensions. This will allow you to make correct judgments as to whether or not the approximations are moving gradually closer to the target behavior. If the behavior is not well defined, reinforcement may be delivered at inappropriate steps and you may be inadvertently reinforcing approximations away from the goal.

The shaping of behaviors may be useful when target behaviors are preceded by clearly identifiable precursors, as well as when the problem behavior varies widely on some dimension of intensity or duration. Shaping is a gradual process which can be time consuming and the effects of which can be delayed. Once achieved, however, the effects are long lasting.

The following are some case examples where shaping procedures were used effectively:

- Harry had considerable difficulty talking in a normal tone. His voice was loud and consequently disruptive in several environments. A shaping procedure was implemented to reinforce increasingly closer approximations to a natural tone.
- A functional analysis determined that whining verbalizations almost always preceded Jesse's temper tantrums. It was further determined that the tantrums served the communicative function of being a substitute for requesting. A shaping strategy for this problem involved the decision to respond to the whining vocalizations before they escalated into a temper tantrum. Then the reinforcer of responsiveness was used to shape this earlier response to include less whining and more explicitly verbal requests. For example, when Jesse's toy got broken and he began to whine and become angry, the teacher would say, "Jesse, I know it makes you mad that the toy broke. Tell me, 'I'm mad because the toy broke.'"

CHAINING

Sometimes tasks or responses cannot be performed because they require that several different behaviors be combined. An example is washing one's hands. When this is the case a particularly effective way of teaching is through a procedure called *chaining*. This involves teaching a complete *sequence* of behaviors in a particular order.

In the case of washing one's hands, the sequence to be taught would be as follows:

1. Turn on the water
2. Wet hands
3. Pick up soap
4. Lather hands
5. Replace soap
6. Rub hands together
7. Rinse hands

8. Turn off water
9. Get paper towel
10. Dry hands
11. Throw paper towel in trash

Chaining can be used within the discrete-trial format, with a series of behaviors constituting the response desired. The decision as to how much of the chain of behavior is considered to be one response depends upon the individual situation as well as the way in which the task is broken down. This breakdown of task components is known as *task analysis*. It must be conducted *first*, to specify the order of the steps in the sequence. The chaining procedure is then used in actually teaching the sequence in a systematic way.

There are three different chaining strategies, each of which will be discussed in turn: forward chaining, backward chaining, and global chaining.

Forward Chaining

Forward chaining reinforces combinations of behaviors by beginning with the first behavior required by the task and proceeding to the second, third, fourth, and so on.

How to Do It.   The first decision when using forward chaining is whether to do whole-task or step-by-step presentation. In a whole-task presentation, the entire task is presented and the learner is prompted through everything except the step she is performing for reinforcement. In a step-by-step procedure, steps can be presented independently of one another. The decision regarding which to use is usually determined by the task itself and by the most sensible procedure. In the hand-washing example, it is clear that this chain must be presented as a whole task. It would be awkward and in some ways impossible to present the steps independently of one another. One could not lather one's hands without first wetting them and then picking up the soap.

After making the decision regarding presentation, the next step is to conduct a good task analysis. Once the steps are clearly delineated, they are taught in the natural order of their occurrence in the performance of the task (see Figure 3.9).

When to Use It.   Forward chaining should be used with learners who learn best when there is a sequential order to be followed and with tasks

Step 1: Get books

Step 2: Get knapsack

Step 3: Put books in knapsack

Step 4: Put knapsack on

FIGURE 3.9. Teaching the use of a knapsack with forward chaining

that are easier at the beginning of the chain, such as shoe tying, using the telephone, and certain cooking tasks.

Caution. When using forward chaining and whole-task presentation, reinforcement is temporarily removed from the student's response unless social reinforcement is used as part of the teaching sequence. Social reinforcement may or may not be a natural part of the sequence.

Backward Chaining

Backward chaining involves teaching a complete sequence of behaviors that must be performed in a particular order, starting with the last step and working backward to the first.

How to Do It. As with forward chaining, the first decision is whether to use whole-task or step-by-step presentation, and the same rules hold in making the decision. Again, the next step is to conduct a good task analysis. Once the steps are clearly delineated, they are presented in reverse order. Thus you would begin with the last step, then teach the next-to-last step, then the third-to-last step, and so on. An example of this procedure is shown in Figure 3.10.

When to Use It. Use backward chaining with learners who need immediate reinforcement and who like to see the task completed. It should be used with tasks in which the easiest steps are at the end of the chain, such as using zippers, making toast, setting the table, and performing certain assembly tasks.

FIGURE 3.10.   Teaching the making of juice with backward chaining

Caution.   The staff member or trainer must be there to initiate the activity.

Global Chaining

Global chaining is one more way of teaching component parts of a task, then chaining them together. The difference with global chaining is that you don't need to start at either the beginning or the end of the sequence. You can choose to teach a step or steps in the middle, if those are what you've determined to be the easiest steps of the task. Then you might use backward chaining to get to the beginning. Or, you might teach, for example, steps 1 to 4 and then skip to step 6, and so on.

How to Do It.   As with the other two chaining procedures, the first decision is whether to use whole-task or step-by-step presentation. Then you need to conduct a good task analysis. In global chaining, the first steps taught are the easiest, followed by the more difficult ones.

When to Use It.   Use global chaining with learners who easily become prompt dependent or who are motivated to be independent. It is best used with tasks that are intermittently difficult (e.g., washing dishes) or easier at the beginning and end (e.g., tooth brushing). Figure 3.11 shows how washing dishes might be taught. The easier steps (1, 2, and 4) can be taught first, with the harder ones (3 and 5) saved for later.

Caution.   In global chaining, the learner may not perceive the task steps as being sequential, so it likely will take longer for her to learn the

Step 1: Fill sink with soap & water — easy teach early

Step 2: Put dishes in — easy teach early

Step 3: Wash dishes — hard wait until later

Step 4: Rinse dishes — easy teach early

Step 5: Stack dishes — hard wait until later

FIGURE 3.11. Teaching dishwashing with global chaining

order of the steps in performing the whole task. The staff member or trainer must be present throughout the entire task.

PRINCIPLE OF PARTIAL PARTICIPATION

Sometimes a learner is not granted the opportunity to participate in a certain task because it appears she will never learn to do it independently. In such a case, the principle of partial participation suggests that she ought to be able at least to participate partially, to the extent of her ability. Often participation is facilitated if the materials, sequences, or rules are changed. These changes are referred to as *adaptations*, and they may be temporary or permanent (as are crutches or prostheses), depending on the needs of the individual and the environments in which she needs to function.

In the preceding chaining examples, staff could use adaptations in teaching some or all of the task. For example, washing dishes is certainly a job that can be done by one person, but it need not be. If a learner is having significant trouble, both the usual procedure and the materials can be adapted, temporarily or permanently. The student could learn, for instance, to hand the dishes to someone else, who puts them in the water and washes and rinses them. The student could then stack them in the dish-drying rack. An alternative would be to teach the student to load a dishwasher.

Adaptations may even allow the learner to perform a task independent-ly. A learner who is very slow in the morning could be taught, for example, to fill a knapsack with his books and other materials after dinner and leave it on the table for the morning. (This is known as sequence adaptation.)

For tooth brushing, the learner could be given a series of pictures and taught to use them as cues for what to do next (materials adaptation). A learner who has great difficulty stirring juice can be taught to put the juice and water into a blender and turn on the blender (materials adaptation).

Adaptations, whether temporary or permanent, are ways of increasing independence and allowing for at least partial participation. The goal is always for independence, however, and adaptations must be chosen care-fully. See the bibliography for suggestions on how to choose adaptations.

4

Prompts and Prompt Fading

A *prompt* is defined as the assistance provided to the learner after the presentation of the instructional stimulus, but *before* the response. This procedure is used to assure a correct response. *Prompt fading* is defined as the systematic reduction of a prompt until it is eliminated or redefined as an integrated part of the task.

DISTINCTION BETWEEN PROMPTING AND CORRECTING

Prompts and correction procedures are often confused. A correction procedure is the assistance or information provided after an incorrect response or a delay in responding. This is clearly distinguished from a prompt, which occurs before the response.

This distinction between prompts and corrections is perhaps more clear when examined within the context of an instructional sequence. Figure 4.1 presents schematic diagrams of both prompts and corrections as they are used in instructional sequences. In the prompting sequence a specific scenario might include the following:

> *Stimulus/Instruction:* A stack of plates is presented, with the words, "Set the table, please."
> *Prompt:* Teacher immediately guides the learner to the placement of each plate on the table.
> *Correct response:* Learner places the plates correctly.
> *Consequence/Reinforcer:* Teacher says, "Thank you."

In any instructional sequence, the learner may respond incorrectly, by doing the "wrong" thing or by not doing the correct thing quickly enough.

FIGURE 4.1.   Instructional sequences for prompting and correcting
procedures

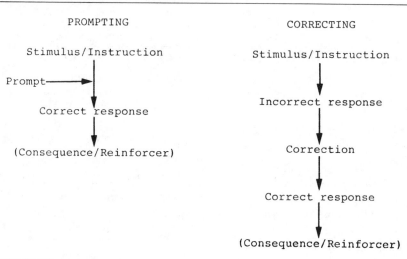

In the correction-strategy sequence a specific scenario might resemble either of the following:

> *Stimulus/Instruction:* A stack of plates is presented, with the words,
> "Set the table, please."
> *Incorrect response:* Learner puts the plates in the middle of the table.
> *Correction procedure:* Teacher removes the plates, returns them to the
> learner, points to where the plates belong, and repeats the in-
> struction.
> *Correct response:* Learner puts the plates in the correct place.
> *Consequence/Reinforcer:* Teacher says, "Thank you."

> *Stimulus/Instruction:* A stack of plates is presented, with the words,
> "Set the table, please."
> *Incorrect response:* Learner puts the plates in the middle of the table.
> *Correction procedure:* Teacher removes the plates, returns them to the
> student, points to where the plates belong, and repeats the in-
> struction.
> *Incorrect response:* Learner stands motionless, holding the plates in
> his hand.
> *Correction procedure:* Teacher points again to the place where the
> plates belong and repeats the instruction.

Incorrect response: Learner places the plates incorrectly.

Correction procedure: Teacher picks up the plates, puts them in the correct place, repeats the instruction, and gives the plates back to the student.

Correct response: Learner puts the plates in the right spot.

Consequence/Reinforcer: Teacher says, "Thank goodness!"

The second example is all too common in classrooms and other settings for learners with exceptional needs. Fortunately, most learners adapt well to such a strategy and ultimately learn to do the task correctly and independently. For some learners, however, there is danger in positively reinforcing a correct response when it has been obtained through a correction procedure. The danger lies in the fact that the incorrect response also may become reinforced and become part of the response chain (see chapter 3). Table 4.1 contrasts what occurs under the two conditions, prompting and correcting. As can be seen, there are numerous reasons why prompting may be the better procedure, although it is not necessarily always to be preferred. Most of us learn well through corrections, and they occur often in everyday life. When an individual appears to be "hooked" on the help given by staff, however, it becomes especially important to consider using a prompt rather than a correction. Over time he may be able to tolerate a more natural teaching style.

SUGGESTIONS FOR IMPLEMENTING PROMPTS AND PROMPT FADING

General Considerations

Type of Prompt. All types of prompts are used in instructional programming. Prompts can be verbal, physical, or visual, or within the stimulus itself. They should be determined by the individual needs of the learner and the requirements of the task.

Timing the Prompt. The crucial factor in the timing of prompts is that they should always come immediately following the stimulus or natural cue and before an error can occur.

How to Fade. Fading of any type of prompt should always be done gradually and systematically. Fading too quickly can result in confusion and possible loss of the skill for the student, while fading too slowly may

TABLE 4.1.   Contrasting results of the use of prompting and correcting procedures

Prompting	Correcting
Learner learns to respond to first S^D presented.	Learner may be confused about which part of the chain is the "real" S^D.
Learner never has to wait for assistance; it's automatic.	Learner may learn to wait for assistance or correction before he responds.
Learner is reinforced only for distinctly correct response.	Learner may be reinforced for mistake in chain, as well as for correct response.
Learner is less likely to "hook" onto or become dependent upon assistance, as prompt and fade are planned in advance and adapted to the student's learning style.	Learner may "hook" onto correction procedure and expect that it is supposed to be there as the "next step."
A support person can monitor own behavior and more easily tell what went wrong right away.	A support person may not be aware that he inadvertently is including new steps in the behavioral chain.
Learners with severe defects that result in poor understanding of social information can more readily understand what actions of theirs have which effects. This helps them understand cause and effect better.	Learners who have poor social-interaction skills may not be able to tell a correction from an instruction or an attempt to give a reinforcer.

result in boredom (and perhaps problem behaviors). Use the following suggestions:

1. Always fade to the most natural cue.
2. Know how to fade out a prompt before you put it in.
3. Be systematic.
4. Be flexible.
5. Monitor carefully.
6. Communicate the level of fade to others using the prompt.
7. Consider the need for the learner to be able to generalize.
8. In situations that are not dangerous, try "probing" (see next paragraph) to assess the learner's level of independence.
9. As always, *individualize*. Some learners do well with corrections, while others respond best to verbal prompts. Decisions about what procedures to do and when and where must be based on individual differences.

Use of Probes.   How quickly students will learn about and respond to prompts is never predictable. Sometimes they learn more rapidly than we expect. In such situations we may want periodically to "probe" to see how much the learner can do independently. You probe by rapidly fading or even withholding the prompt occasionally. Remember, it is important to record probes and their results.

Specific Types of Prompts and Prompt Fading

Verbal Prompts.   Use verbal prompts for tasks that are usually performed with verbal direction, but be sure the language is understood by the learner. Verbal prompts may be direct ("Punch your time card") or indirect ("What do you do next?"). Verbal prompts are the most common, probably because they are so natural. They often work well, with the learner becoming truly independent.

Verbal prompts are very difficult to fade for some learners, however. Fading is done either by reducing the intensity or the directness of the verbal prompt. Verbal prompts should be used with caution with learners with severe communication disabilities, as they easily become prompt dependent.

Physical Prompts.   Physical prompts involve actually moving the learner and include direct hand-over-hand guidance. They are best suited for tasks that ultimately should be done independently. The prompt should be directive enough to generate a correct response, but it should never be so strong that the learner is being physically forced to respond. We are suggesting directed and careful guidance, *not* forced responding. If a learner resists a physical prompt, another type should be used.

Fading should be done gradually and should be performance based, not time determined. Fading is done by decreasing the amount of assistance provided, in terms of the degree of movement provided or in terms of where the prompt is given, or both. Figure 4.2 shows the fading of physical prompting in guiding a learner to his seat. The original prompt, an arm around the shoulders, is faded to less and less contact and finally to no touch at all.

Visual Prompts.   Visual prompts include gestures, pictures, demonstrations or modeling, and proximity cues. Many learners have difficulty "reading" non-verbal communication and need exaggerated facial or gestural cues. Other individuals may rely on gestures that inadvertently convey the correct response. Figure 4.3 shows an example of such an instance, in which the teacher's point implies the answer. A learner may "hook" on

Target Behavior: Matt takes his seat independently.

Arm around   Hand on   Hand on   Walk over
 shoulder   back   elbow   together

FIGURE 4.2.   Fading a physical prompt

such an inadvertent prompt, and when it is no longer available, she can not do the task. Often the learner then uses inappropriate behavior to express confusion, and staff think she is "noncompliant."

The major kinds of visual prompts and some guidelines for their use are as follows:

> *Pictures:* These are appropriate for learners with low language ability, though some symbol representation abilities are required. They also help with learners who have sequencing problems.
>
> *Demonstration:* This is appropriate for learners with good imitation skills and social awareness. Other learners can be used effectively as models. Demonstration often requires exaggerated cues.
>
> *Proximity:* This type of cue is appropriate for learners who depend on visual and spatial information. An example of this is a staff member teaching students to clean the sink. He wanted them to be able to perform the whole task independently, beginning with gathering the cleaning materials. To prompt this, he began by placing the materials very close to the sink, then gradually moved the materials away and finally into the cabinet.

Fading depends on the type of visual prompt. Use the following suggestions:

> *Gestures:* These are easily faded by decreasing the intensity of movement and position of gestures.

FIGURE 4.3.   Avoid inappropriate gestural cues

Pictures: Fade these by decreasing their use. If fading is impossible, the pictures may become a permanent adaptation.

Demonstration: These should be faded to indirect verbal prompts or gestures. Again, gestures are preferred over verbal prompts for some learners.

Proximity: Gradually fade physical proximity to the learner.

Sometimes the physical proximity of the staff member to the learner may be an inadvertent prompt. Remember, true independence can occur only when the staff person involved has been completely faded out of the situation, unless he has a specific reason for being a part of it.

Within-Stimulus Prompts.   Within-stimulus prompts are among the most effective to use, but they are often difficult to engineer. A within-stimulus prompt is one in which the critical dimension of the stimulus is exaggerated. So, if the critical dimension is size, initially the size variation would be exaggerated; if the critical dimension is color, color would be varied. In the following examples, proximity and size are the critical dimensions:

- *Proximity.* Mr. Braswell wanted Patrick to learn to take food only from his own plate, as Patrick was in the habit of grabbing anything within arm's reach. Mr. Braswell used a within-stimulus prompt by exaggerating the dimension of proximity. Each time he and Patrick sat down for a meal, Mr. Braswell sat at the opposite end of the table from Patrick. Patrick earned points toward a special dessert for eating only his own food. Mr. Braswell gradually moved himself and his food closer to Patrick, until he was sitting next to him. Patrick continued to receive points for eating only his own food.

- *Size.* June needed to learn to sort the silverware in her kitchen. Since the critical dimension for this sort is size, June's initial training involved use of a within-stimulus prompt where size was exaggerated. Most spoons June had to sort were teaspoons and soup spoons, but her training began by having her sort very large serving spoons and small espresso spoons (Figure 4.4, A). Once she was successful at sorting these, the espresso spoons were replaced by regular teaspoons and she learned to sort the teaspoons from the serving spoons (Figure 4.4, B). When she could do that sorting task, the serving spoons were replaced by the soup spoons (Figure 4.4, C).

When fading a within-stimulus prompt, always fade along the dimension chosen and always fade gradually.

CONCLUSION

To summarize, there are several advantages to using a prompt over a correction procedure for some learners:

1. It increases the likelihood that the learner is responding to your instruction.
2. It decreases the possibility of students becoming prompt (or correction) dependent.
3. The reinforcement or consequence more clearly relates to the behavior.
4. A prompt provides clearer feedback to the learner.
5. It provides clearer feedback to the staff member or trainer.
6. It enables you to monitor your own behavior better.

There are some cautions to bear in mind when using any prompt, correction, or adaptation. First, behavior problems often occur when assistance provided is no longer available. This typically happens when one staff member provides cues not known to the rest. The client may be waiting for

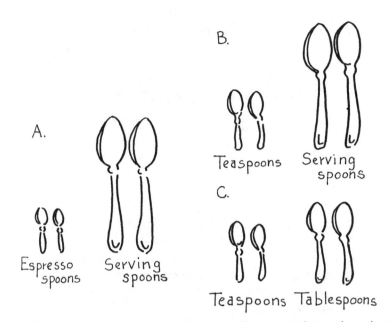

FIGURE 4.4. An example of within-stimulus prompting using size as the critical dimension

the new staff person to say, "What do you do next?" or provide another gesture or aid. New staff, however, think the learner is being noncompliant, and a problem situation soon develops. All prompts, corrections, and adaptations must be purposeful (not inadvertent) and used consistently, particularly with new tasks.

Second, staff are often advised to use "prompt hierarchies," that is, lists of different levels of assistance. Often programs evaluate success by movement along such hierarchies. In fact, as with most things, levels of assistance must be determined individually. With some learners you can fade from verbal assistance to none. Others will think your verbal help is part of the task, and you will have great difficulty fading it. The same is true for gestures, physical help, and other types of prompts. If you use a hierarchy, determine it for each individual and each situation.

5

Data Recording

Data recording forms the basis of the evaluation methods used to draw conclusions about behavior change and involves the objective measurement of behavior over time. Basically, data provide a measure of how often and/or how long an individual engages in a particular behavior. These measures are required in order to choose the most effective change procedure and to indicate if, when, and how much change is occurring.

Many staff members approach data recording or data collection procedures with skepticism and reluctance; however, in working with learners who present severe behavioral challenges, it is essential to implement accurate data collection procedures. This chapter will describe the most widely used methods of recording data. Accurate and ongoing data recording provides at least the following:

1. Systematic and precise observation and measurement of behavior, which will assist staff in determining the most effective way to change or alter a behavior
2. An accurate determination of the effect of a particular behavior change program
3. Assistance in remaining objective
4. A record of behavior that is not influenced by our personal involvement with and/or opinions about individuals or situations
5. A more efficient and accurate manner for pinpointing the moment when progress was interrupted
6. A routine for detecting a specific problem and quickly prescribing remedial action
7. A way to analyze the success of the behavior change program
8. An objective record of behavior that has actually occurred, which relieves us from trying to remember what has occurred or from guessing at the current severity of a behavior

9. An opportunity to detect even very gradual change and progress

Even though we are stressing data collection for problem behavior, data on instructional progress is equally essential and may produce additional clues regarding the problem behavior.

BASELINE DATA

Before initiating any type of behavior change program, it is essential to have information regarding the occurrence of the behavior to be changed, under current conditions. This information is called *baseline data*, and it is gathered by recording the occurrence of a particular response prior to implementing a behavior change program. Baseline data can reveal how severe a behavior is and whether or not intervention is even necessary. Also, if you are trying to teach a new skill, baseline data can indicate the level at which the learner is currently performing. Often, unconventional responses or desired behaviors may occur less frequently or more frequently than you think they do. Taking baseline data will give you an accurate measure of what typically occurs in a specific situation and help you determine what the goals for change should be.

When collecting baseline information, it is essential to remember the following points:

1. Current programming does *not* need to be dropped.
2. Collect baseline data in environments and under learning situations that are as natural as possible.
3. Compare current baseline data with measures of behavior under previous programs, to provide additional clues as to the most effective change program.
4. Use baseline data as a measure against which to compare hypotheses that test the possible communicative functions of the behavior.
5. Obtain a stable baseline before beginning intervention; that is, gather enough data so that range, rate, and variability of behavior are clear. Figure 5.1 shows four plots of baseline data for self-stimulating behavior, but in only two cases have enough data been obtained to show the stable baseline for the number of behaviors exhibited.

The following examples illustrate the need for and usefulness of collecting baseline data:

- Tina engaged in stereotypic behavior. Prior to collecting baseline information, the staff believed she did it "all the time." Once a

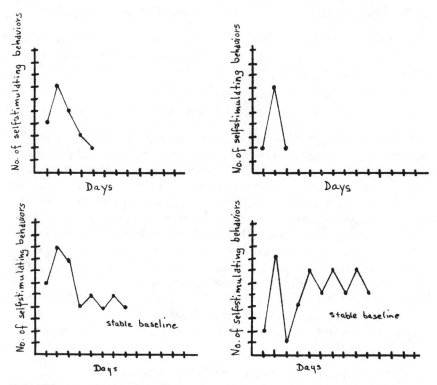

FIGURE 5.1. Examples of graphs of baseline data for self-stimulating behavior

baseline was actually taken, it became obvious that the target behavior occurred less frequently than had been reported and that it
usually occurred only when Tina was bored.

- Jeff's "talking-out" behavior was not perceived by his classroom
  teacher as a disruptive occurrence. On the other hand, the classroom aide complained that it seemed to be a problem in every
  aspect of his day. Baseline data were taken across several settings,
  revealing that Jeff's talking-out behavior was enough of a problem
  that an intervention was necessary. Staff hypothesized that he
  talked out when he was confused or didn't know an answer and that
  he therefore needed a less disruptive and more conventional way of
  asking for assistance.

PROBES

A probe is a return to baseline conditions for several trials or some other brief period, to determine if the learner can progress more quickly than anticipated. It may be that the intervention has already been successful and need not be continued, or can be modified. Probes can be given at the beginning of each step of the program, to determine the necessity of taking the next step. They can also be used to determine if a certain behavior has generalized to another setting.

DATA RECORDING TECHNIQUES

The selection of a data collection system is the first step in the evaluation process. The individual characteristics of the collection system selected must be fitted to the observed behavior, to the kind of behavior change desired, and to the kind of information required for decision making. For example, event recording would distinguish the number of times a behavior occurs, while duration data show how long it goes on. The following techniques are some of the most common and efficient for recording behavior.

Event Recording.   Event recording is a method by which a complete record of discrete responses is collected, thus providing an account of the frequency at which a particular behavior occurs. Every time a specific behavior occurs during a predetermined time period, a mark on a piece of paper or a click on a counter is made. This method of data recording can accurately measure a learner's rate of working, hitting, talking, and so forth; and it is appropriate for any behavior where duration is not of concern. The key is being able to define the response or behavior in a way that it can be observed as a discrete event, as in the following example:

- Chuck worked at a cafeteria, making omelets. His employer was not satisfied with the rate at which Chuck worked and decided that, in order to keep the job, Chuck would have to increase his rate of filling omelet orders. The job was broken down into 20-minute intervals in which Chuck was expected to make a certain number of omelets. The boss used event recording to determine how many omelets Chuck made in 20 minutes.

Duration Recording.   Duration recording is a method that measures the total time (out of a designated time period) during which an individual is engaged in a particular response. Although we want to be aware of how often the response occurs, this measure is best used when the main concern is the amount of time someone spends doing something, rather than how often it is done. Tantrums, staying on task, and conventional play behavior are examples of behaviors whose duration can be measured.

Recording is typically done with the aid of a stopwatch. Depending upon the behavior, you may be concerned only with total time per specified period, or you may be interested in the total time of one episode of the behavior. Again, the behavior itself and the planned goal will help determine which measure you plan to use. Here are two examples:

- Sam spent much of his time playing alone. Staff wanted to increase the time he spent playing with others; therefore, they used duration as a data recording system. For one week staff recorded the total amount of time he spent interacting with peers during a specified 30-minute period.
- Lee was prone to having tantrums. Sometimes his tantrums were short but intense. Sometimes they were less intense but lasted for a very long period of time. Staff decided that a combination of frequency and duration data was required, and that they needed to look at the possible communicative functions of Lee's tantrums. Their baseline data and their hypothesis testing indicated that, when Lee was asked to do something in which he was not interested, his tantrums were short but intense, communicating a loud, "I don't want to do this!" However, when what he was asked to do made sense to him but he didn't know how to do it, his tantrums were less intense but longer. This was seen as a somewhat extended, "Please, somebody help me figure this out!"

Time Sampling.   Time sampling is a direct observational method of collecting data in which the observer records, in short intervals, the presence or absence of the behaviors to be changed. This method divides each observation session into a number of equal intervals, with the target behavior being observed only for a brief period at the end of each interval. This technique is generally more sensitive to subtle, hard-to-observe behaviors. The period of observation may be 10 seconds, 5 seconds, or even 2 seconds every so many minutes, depending on the nature and average occurrence of the response. At the end of each interval, the observer indicates on a sheet of paper whether or not the designated behavior occurred.

Time sampling can be used efficiently in situations where you are engaged in other activities. You simply check at the end of every interval to record the presence or absence of the behavior, as in the following example:
- Kevin often hit his head. In order to get a better sense of how often and in what environments this occurred, Kevin's classroom and

vocational teachers and his group home parents all took data. At the end of every 10 minutes they observed him for 1 minute. If the behavior did not occur during that minute, at the end of the interval the data sheet was marked with a minus sign (−). If it did occur, the data sheet was marked with a plus sign (+), regardless of how often it occurred during that minute. Figure 5.2 shows how the data sheet looked for this activity.

The data recorded from time sampling were used to test some hypotheses regarding the reasons for Kevin's behavior. The data showed that Kevin was hitting his head only during transitions from one activity or environment to another, indicating his confusion about what was going to happen next.

Scatter-Plot Data.   Scatter-plot data collection is a method of recording and/or graphing the day and time of a behavior's occurrence, across a number of environmental variables, in an effort to identify possible characteristics of the environment that might contribute to the behavior's occurrence or nonoccurrence. The method works best when the learner has a relatively constant weekly schedule within the context of a stable staffing pattern. Amy's case serves as an example:

- A scatter-plot analysis (see Figure 5.3) of Amy's tantrums during school hours showed that most tantrums occurred during the late morning hours leading up to lunch. The only hours totally free of tantrums were from 8 to 9 in the morning and from 12 to 1 in the afternoon, right after breakfast and lunch, respectively. This suggested that tantrums were related to food intake. Staff decided to try giving Amy a healthful snack at midmorning and midafternoon. Her tantrums decreased.

Anecdotal Data Recording.   Anecdotal data recording is a method of descriptively recording the response emitted by the learner, the responses of others, and information about the environment (see Figure 5.4). Generally, information should be as objective as possible, although it can include

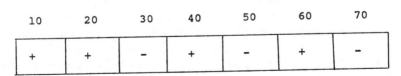

FIGURE 5.2.   Time sampling of head-banging behavior for 60 seconds per 10-minute interval

Tantrums

Scatter Plot Data for Three Weeks

	Mon.	Tues.	Wed.	Thur.	Fri.
8 to 9 A.M.	O	O	O	O	O
9 to 10 A.M.	/	O	/	/	O
10 to 11 A.M.	///	//	//	//	///
11 to 12 P.M.	//	///	/	////	/
12 to 1 P.M.	O	O	O	O	O
1 to 2 P.M.	O	/	/	O	/
2 to 3 P.M.	O	O	O	/	/

FIGURE 5.3. Amy's tantrums: Scatter-plot data for 3 weeks

some impressions. This method is best used to back up other data recording techniques and to enhance data on programs that are using shaping procedures. In shaping procedures it is often difficult to define discrete steps, but anecdotal data recording can help staff to discern specific changes.

A descriptive system is also useful in identifying both the variables influencing a learner's performance and the possible communicative functions of behavior. In addition, anecdotal data can be used to obtain information about incorrect responses, especially regarding the learner's understanding or perception of the situation. Finally, this kind of data can be useful in

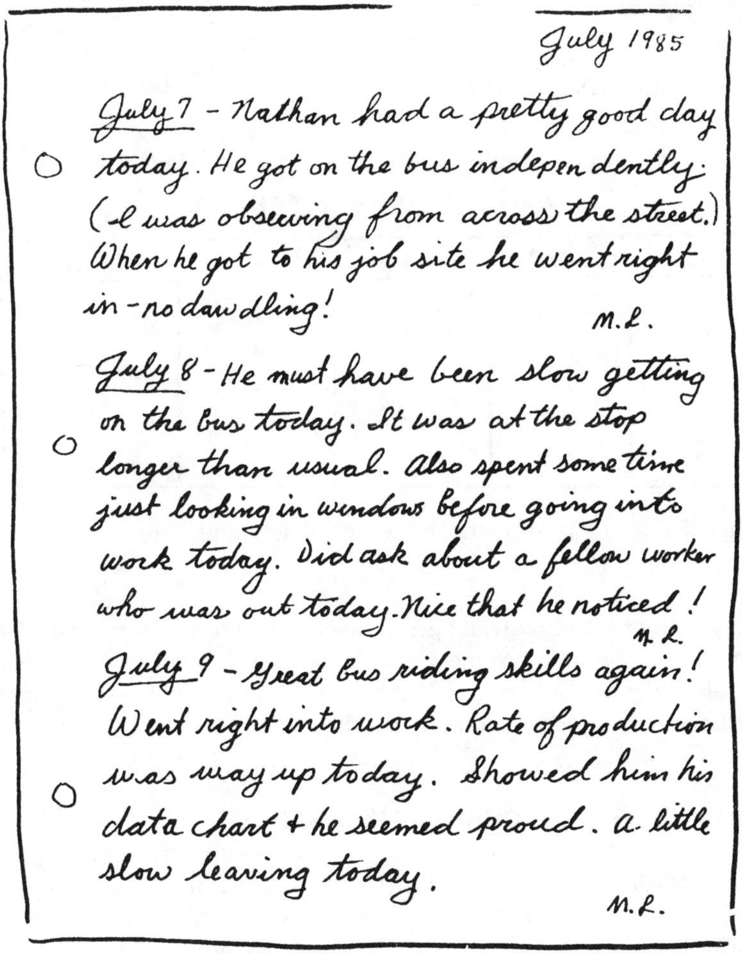

July 1985

July 7 - Nathan had a pretty good day today. He got on the bus independently. (I was observing from across the street.) When he got to his job site he went right in - no dawdling! M.L.

July 8 - He must have been slow getting on the bus today. It was at the stop longer than usual. Also spent some time just looking in windows before going into work today. Did ask about a fellow worker who was out today. Nice that he noticed! M.L.

July 9 - Great bus riding skills again! Went right into work. Rate of production was way up today. Showed him his data chart + he seemed proud. A little slow leaving today. M.L.

FIGURE 5.4. Sample anecdotal data

looking at the overall behavioral repertoire and environmental variables, rather than only discrete instances.

Trial-by-Trial Data. In using the trial-by-trial method of data recording, data are collected at the end of each discrete trial (as in the discrete-trial format discussed in chapter 3). Scoring indicates whether the response was correct, incorrect, or correct with prompts (see Figure 5.5). When teaching most behaviors (e.g., discrimination tasks, self-help skills), a rec-

Student: Mary			Starting date: 9/14	
Teacher: Miss Grundy			Time: 10:00 A.M.	
Behavior: Mary will put her tennis shoes on at gym time, without request.				
Day	Correct	Incorrect	Prompt	Comments
1	x		x	
2		x	x	
3	x		x	
4	x			
5		x		
6		x	x	

FIGURE 5.5.   Trial-by-trial data recording sheet

ord of a learner's trial-by-trial performance will indicate how the student is progressing. Such data are most efficiently recorded during the intertrial interval, which is also a convenient time to enhance trial-by-trial data by recording some anecdotal data, as just described.

CHARTS AND GRAPHS

Data collection is obviously of little use if there is no convenient way of referring to it. Charts and graphs that provide a visual summary of how behavior has or has not changed over time are essential.

There are an infinite number of possible charting schemes. You will probably be using charts and graphs entered on standard, squared graph paper. The vertical axis is used to indicate the level of the behavior, measured in percentage of frequency or number of discrete events. The horizontal axis refers to time, in days, in half-hour training sessions, or some other measure. Keep up with graphing and charting on a regular basis. This will facilitate tracking progress and noting the need for program change at critical periods.

6

Differential Reinforcement of Other Behavior

Differential reinforcement of other behavior (DRO) is reinforcement for not engaging in the target behavior for a specified interval of time, regardless of what other responses occur or do not occur during this period. The following examples illustrate this procedure:

- Sue was allowed to have a video of her choice on Saturday if she did not cut any classes that entire week.
- Tom received extra juice and time with the teacher each morning and afternoon in which he did not have a tantrum.
- Donna was trying to lose weight. She made up a schedule for herself in which she put money into a special clothing account for every week she did not eat sweets and/or junk food.

These learners will be "paid off" for the absence of these behaviors, even if other problem behaviors occur during the interval. For example, if the student *does not* have a tantrum but *does* engage in self-stimulatory behavior, he still receives his juice at the end of the morning and afternoon.

VARIATIONS OF *DRO* SCHEDULES

The following discussion gives four variations of the DRO schedule and an example of each in an applied situation. For the sake of comparison, the examples are in 1-hour intervals where possible. As we will discuss later, the interval is determined by the baseline frequency of the behavior, naturally occurring break times, and other factors. In our experience successful DRO procedures have utilized intervals ranging from a few minutes to several weeks. The variations to be discussed include:

DRO reset schedules
DRO fixed-interval schedules
DRO increasing-interval schedules
DRO progressive (DROP) schedules

Teachers often express concern that students with severe handicaps will not "understand" the DRO schedule. In fact, these procedures were developed for use in laboratories with animals. It is not necessary for students to understand contingencies "verbally," in order for the procedures to work; indeed, the effects are better if students are helped to understand. We have included suggestions for giving students concrete feedback that will make contingencies clearer.

DRO Reset Schedules.   In the DRO reset procedure, the interval timer is reset each time the response target behavior occurs. For example, it was used in a case where the target behavior was assaultive actions and the specified interval was 1 hour. The student, George, was presented with reinforcement at the end of every hour in which an assault had not occurred. Figure 6.1 shows the DRO reset schedule for this program, partially filled out for day 1. As the schedule shows, there was no assaultive behavior between 9:00 and 10:00 A.M., so reinforcement (S^{R+}) was delivered at 10:00. Likewise, there was no occurrence between 10:00 and 11:00, or between 11:00 and 12:00, so reinforcement was also delivered at 11:00 and 12:00. If no assaults had occurred the entire day, reinforcement would have been given every hour on the hour.

When an assault does occur, regardless of what time it is, the timer is reset, and a new 1-hour interval starts. Examples of this are given in Figure

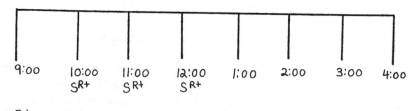

FIGURE 6.1.   DRO reset schedule for reinforcement at 1-hour intervals, with no occurrence of target behavior

6.2. On this particular day, at 10:15 A.M., George hit another student. As a result, he did not get his reinforcer at 11:00, and the 1-hour interval was reset to begin at 10:15. After an hour he had not hit again, so at 11:15 he received a reinforcer, and again at 12:15. When he hit again at 12:50, he missed his 1:15 reinforcer, and the 1-hour interval was reset to begin at 12:50.

DRO Fixed-Interval Schedules.   In the DRO fixed-interval procedure, the interval schedule is fixed, and reinforcement is delivered at the end of each interval during which the response does not occur. The procedure differs from the reset schedule in that the interval time is not reset with each occurrence of target behavior. As an example, we will use Lynn's case, where the target behavior was tantrums and the specified interval was 1 hour. Reinforcement was presented on the hour, every hour in which no temper tantrum occurred.

The results of this program are shown in Figure 6.3, for one day. As can be seen, there were no temper tantrums between the hours of 9:00 and 1:00, so reinforcement was given at 10:00, 11:00, 12:00, and 1:00. But at 1:30 Lynn had a tantrum; therefore, at 2:00 no reinforcement was delivered. There was no tantrum between 2:00 and 3:00, so at 3:00 reinforcement was delivered. Another tantrum occurred between 3:00 and 4:00, so there was no reinforcement at 4:00. Note that in a fixed interval like this, because the clock is not reset, one tantrum may cause the student to wait almost 2 hours without reinforcement, if that tantrum occurs soon after reinforcement delivery.

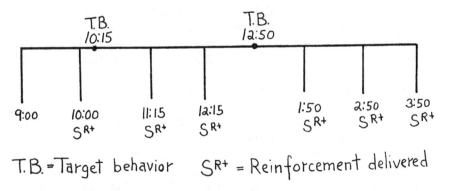

T.B. = Target behavior S^{R+} = Reinforcement delivered

FIGURE 6.2.   DRO reset schedule for reinforcement at 1-hour intervals, with target behavior occurring twice

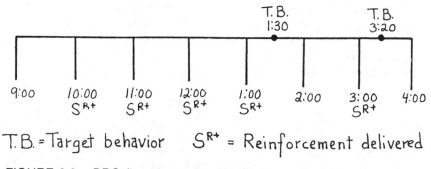

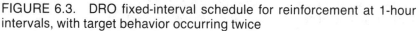

FIGURE 6.3.   DRO fixed-interval schedule for reinforcement at 1-hour intervals, with target behavior occurring twice

DRO Increasing-Interval Schedules.   A DRO increasing-interval schedule is one way of *thinning* or *fading* the reinforcement by gradually increasing the interval size. If the specified interval passes without a target response occurring, reinforcement is delivered and the next interval could be increased by a certain amount of time. If the response does occur, however, the next interval would stay the same. In Figure 6.4, the target behavior was aggression. Beginning on day 10, the interval was increased by 15-minute increments each time two consecutively successful intervals passed. There was, however, no more than one increase made per day. On day 11, the aggressive behavior occurred several times; therefore, there was no increase in the interval size. On day 12 there were two consecutive intervals (of 75 minutes) where no aggression occurred. After those two intervals, the time was increased to 90 minutes and then to 105 minutes.

As you increase the interval size, you may want to increase the amount of reinforcement that can be earned for each successful interval in such a way that the total reinforcement available in a day is not dramatically reduced. This would avoid the countertherapeutic effect of a person being penalized (getting less reinforcement) as her behavior comes more and more under control. Reinforcement should be faded *very* gradually.

DRO Progressive Schedules.   In a DRO progressive (DROP) schedule, the interval size remains the same. The amount or kind of reinforcement increases as the student controls the undesirable behavior for more and more consecutive intervals. For example, 8-year-old Pat received colorful stickers to add to his collection when he did not yell in class. He earned one sticker for the first hour of not yelling out in class, two stickers for the second consecutive hour, three for the third consecutive hour, and three

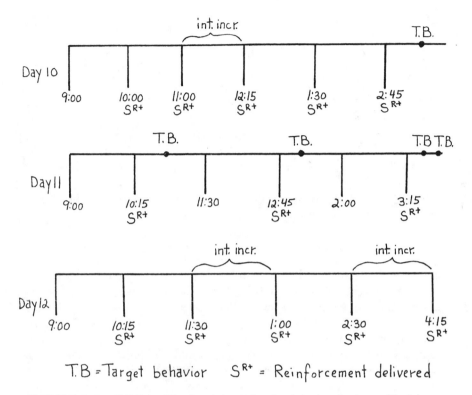

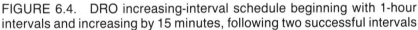

T.B = Target behavior   S^{R+} = Reinforcement delivered

FIGURE 6.4.   DRO increasing-interval schedule beginning with 1-hour intervals and increasing by 15 minutes, following two successful intervals

stickers thereafter for every consecutive hour with no occurrence of the behavior. If the behavior occurred, however, he received *no* sticker for that hour and the following hour he was "recycled"; that is, he started over at one sticker per hour. The reinforcement schedule for one day is shown in Figure 6.5. No yelling occurred during the hours of 9:00 and 1:00, so Pat progressed to the maximum reinforcement. When yelling occurred between 1:00 and 2:00, he received nothing at 2:00. No yelling occurred between 2:00 and 3:00, so, as the figure shows, he began again by receiving one sticker.

A never-ending progression of increasing reinforcers is unrealistic, so a limit must be determined by observing the "free access" rule. When designing any reinforcement schedule one must consider how much an individual would want of a particular reinforcement if there were no limits on avail-

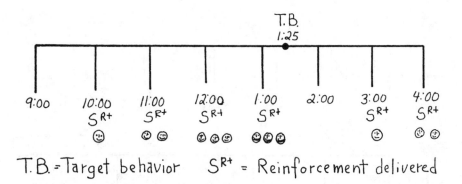

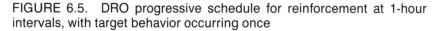

FIGURE 6.5.   DRO progressive schedule for reinforcement at 1-hour intervals, with target behavior occurring once

ability. This is particularly important with progressively increasing schedules of reinforcement such as DROP. Using the free access rule, the maximum amount of a reinforcer available to the individual should still be less than that which he would seek if he had unlimited access to it. For example, suppose a teenage student ordinarily has pizza once every other week but loves pizza above all other food and would probably eat three pizzas per week if he were offered them. Pizza would likely be a good thing to try as a reinforcer as he could earn one or more slices of pizza for every day that goes by without the occurrence of the problem behavior. However, even if he has a perfect week, that is, earns everything he can on the DROP schedule, he should be able to earn no more than about two pizzas per week.

SUGGESTIONS FOR IMPLEMENTING
DRO PROCEDURES

Before implementing a DRO schedule, the following variables must be addressed to assure that the procedure is implemented adequately and in the most effective manner possible:

1. Selection of target behavior
2. Selection of time interval
3. Selection of DRO variation
4. Selection of reinforcers
5. Fading of reinforcers

6. Positive programming
7. Target behavior occurrence

Selection of Target Behavior.   Many times a staff member is faced with a learner who has a large number of inappropriate behaviors. In such a case, perhaps the best practice is to list the problem behaviors according to their level of seriousness and to target one or two of the most serious for the DRO schedule. By doing this, of course, there is a chance that you might inadvertently reinforce another inappropriate behavior. Such inadvertent reinforcement could be prevented, however, by placing the reinforcer on "limited hold" for a short period of time immediately following the occurrence of an inappropriate behavior. For example, if the inappropriate behaviors include physical aggression and cursing, we would likely choose physical aggression as the priority behavior, recognizing that we would not simultaneously be reducing cursing. If, however, we delayed the reinforcement for no occurrence of the priority behavior until at least 5 minutes have passed with no cursing, then the secondary behavior would not be immediately reinforced.

A sample chart of such a situation is given in Figure 6.6. There was no aggression or cursing between 9:00 and 10:00, so reinforcement was delivered. Aggression occurred between 10:00 and 11:00, and, even though there was no cursing, no reinforcement was delivered, as the targeted behavior was aggression. Between 12:00 and 1:00, there was no aggression, but at 12:59 the learner cursed. The limited hold procedure was used to delay reinforcement for no aggression until 5 minutes after the secondary behavior (i.e., cursing) occurred.

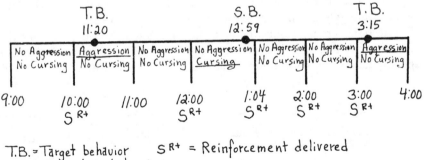

FIGURE 6.6.   DRO fixed-interval schedule used with limited hold procedure to avoid reinforcement of secondary behavior

T.B. 10:10		T.B. 11:25	T.B. 11:45		T.B. 1:40

No Hitting No Throwing No Cursing	No Hitting Throwing No Cursing	Hitting Throwing No Cursing	No Hitting No Throwing No Cursing	Hitting No Throwing No Cursing	No Hitting No Throwing No Cursing

9:00   10:00   11:00   12:00   1:00   2:00   3:00
              S^{R+} S^{R+} S^{R+}

T.B. = Target behavior S^{R+} = Reinforcement delivered

FIGURE 6.7.   DRO fixed-interval schedule combining several problem behaviors into a single response class

Another possibility would be to combine a number of problem behaviors into a single response class. Thus, for delivery of reinforcement to occur, the specified interval would have to pass without any of the identified behaviors occurring. Figure 6.7 shows an example of such a schedule; the response class identified in this case included hitting others, throwing things at people, and cursing. While this procedure can work well in many instances, it is often more difficult to implement with students who are at lower cognitive functioning levels.

Selection of Time Interval.   The selection of an appropriate time interval is vital to successful behavior reduction using a DRO strategy. If the DRO interval selected is too long or too short, the reinforcement schedule will not gain control over the behavior. The interval selected should be based on the interresponse time (IRT) under baseline conditions. The IRT is the average length of time between responses. In the example shown in Figure 6.8, a response occurs 10 times in a 5-hour period, making the average length of time between responses—the IRT—30 minutes. A sensible guideline is to select an interval equal to one-half of the baseline IRT.

$$\text{IRT} = \frac{\text{Observation time}}{\text{Number of responses}} = \frac{5 \text{ hours}}{10 \text{ responses}} = 30 \text{ minutes}$$

$$\text{DRO interval} = \frac{\text{IRT}}{2} = \frac{30 \text{ minutes}}{2} = 15 \text{ minutes}$$

FIGURE 6.8.   Calculating the interresponse time and DRO interval

In this case, the interval would be 15 minutes. This proportion insures that the learner will be reinforced at least 50 percent of the time, assuming baseline rates are fairly stable. (See chapter 5 for discussion of stable baseline rates.)

When determining the appropriate interval size, always remember the "Goldilocks Rule": The interval should not be *too large* or *too small*; it should be *just right*. If the interval is too small, the occurrence of the behavior will not have enough impact on overall density of reinforcement. Losing a few reinforcements out of many won't matter very much to the learner. If the interval size is too large, the learner will have too little opportunity to be reinforced.

Selection of DRO Variations.   There are no well-established guidelines for selecting one DRO variation over another, but you may find the following suggestions helpful:

Fixed-interval schedule: This variation of DRO is primarily used to establish initial control, to avoid reinforcement delivery developing as an S^D for problem behavior, and for behaviors that are fairly evenly distributed and do not aggregate around one or a limited number of situations. This schedule might be used, for example, to control the screaming behavior of a young learner; in such a case, a penny might be an appropriate reinforcer and 1 hour an appropriate interval.

Reset schedule: This variation seems particularly useful for people who tend to engage in high rate problem behavior after a fixed-interval payoff is no longer available. It is often used in combination with the DROP variation. On its own it might be used to control a learner's talking out behavior; a 1-hour interval in which the target behavior did not occur could be reinforced with 5 minutes of free time to be used at the end of the day.

Progressive schedule: The DRO progressive (DROP) variation is particularly useful for low rate behavior or for individuals who require more frequent feedback (i.e., smaller intervals) than would be established under the fixed-interval or reset variations. It is the most powerful variation of DRO. In the example depicted in Figure 6.9, it was used to control cursing by reinforcing each successful 1-hour interval with pennies up to a maximum of three that could be earned at one time. In most cases, however, the maximum is between five and ten units of reinforcement if the full effect of the procedure is to be obtained.

Increasing-interval schedule: This is primarily used to fade out a DRO reinforcement schedule after control has been established, although some people prefer to use this variation to establish initial control.

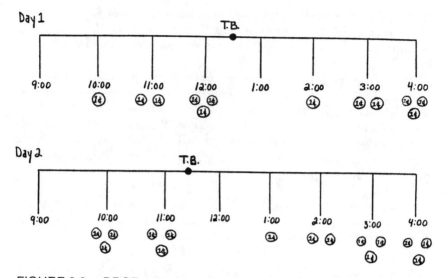

FIGURE 6.9.   DROP schedule with three-unit reinforcement maximum

This schedule might be used to control a behavior like flipping papers; the initial 1-hour interval size would be increased by 15 minutes after two successful intervals, and reinforcement might be tokens that could be exchanged for magazines and other preferred items.

When increasing-interval schedules are used, partial intervals at the end of the day are usually not reinforced. Each day starts with a new interval whose size depends upon whether or not the criterion for increasing the interval size had been reached on the previous day. Performance across days is considered, but only on the basis of complete intervals. It is possible, of course, that two different settings—school and home, for example—would cooperate with a single schedule. Such cooperation requires good communication between settings to assure that changes in the interval size reflect the learner's performance in each setting.

Selection of Reinforcers.   You will need a reinforcer that is at least as powerful as whatever reinforcer seems to be maintaining the problem behavior. In some cases it is possible to identify and employ the same reinforcer that is maintaining the undesired behavior. For example, if a learner throws tantrums in order to receive free time, then free time could be used to reinforce tantrum-free intervals.

Two points should be remembered when choosing the reinforcers. First, the reinforcer selected should be available *only* when the learner meets the criterion under the DRO schedule; if the reinforcer is 1 hour of video games contingent upon 1 week of no fighting, there must be no other access to video games. Second, the total amount of reinforcement earnable should be somewhat less (50%–70%) than what the learner would seek given free access. Thus 1 hour of video games per week will not be an appropriate reinforcer for a learner who would only *choose* to play them 1 hour per month. It may be necessary to select instead a movie, pizza, or something else he would choose perhaps twice a week.

Fading of Reinforcers.   You will want to fade out the DRO procedure once the rate of behavior has reached an acceptable level. Switching over to an increasing-interval or DROP schedule often helps. DROP schedules are particularly powerful and should be considered if the behavior has been reduced, but not to acceptable levels. The following is an example of using a DROP schedule to further reduce a behavior:

- Mr. Hulub used a DRO fixed-interval schedule to get Jimmy's talk-outs down to a more reasonable level. To help Jimmy maintain longer periods of time without any talk-outs, he moved from the fixed schedule to a DRO progressive schedule. In the fixed-interval schedule, Jimmy had received one token for every hour with no talk-outs. In the progressive schedule, he received one token for the first hour and one more for each consecutive hour, up to eight tokens per hour for no talk-outs.

DROP schedules require the use of reinforcers that can be presented in progressively increasing units. Examples include number of tokens, ounces of beverage, or hours of television. The maximum level, achieved under total success, should still be equal to less than the learner would choose given free access, and it should be reasonable in its density.

Positive Programming.   Since DRO does not systematically build or reinforce the occurrence of positive or functional behaviors, it should be used within the context of positive programming. In situations where the learner does not have a variety of appropriate functional skills, the solitary use of a DRO schedule (or DRL; see chapter 7) is specifically not recommended. Rather, these schedules should always be used within the context of positive programming to develop a repertoire of appropriate functional skills to fill the void left by the eliminated behavior. (See the discussion of positive programming in chapter 1.)

Target Behavior Occurrences.   If the target behavior occurs when implementing a DRO schedule, there are a number of options that may be considered:

1. The target response could be ignored.
2. The learner could be given matter-of-fact feedback that the response is unacceptable.
3. A stimulus-change procedure could be used (see chapter 11).
4. In the case of very dangerous and/or destructive behavior, an emergency intervention could be employed.

At no time should the behavior be punished, nor should the learner receive negative feedback when the behavior occurs (e.g., "Oh, you just lost your chance for this hour"). For further information on emergency and crisis interventions, see the bibliography.

CONCLUSION

There are several advantages to using the DRO procedure, including the following:

1. *Lack of behavioral contrast:* In programs designed to reduce problem behavior, one of the goals is to generalize treatment gains across settings. If generalization does not occur and behavior problems that decrease within the treatment setting are found to increase outside of the treatment setting, a behavioral contrast has been produced. Research evidence suggests that DRO does not produce behavioral contrasts, thus presenting a clear advantage over many other procedures.
2. *Few, if any, negative side effects:* DRO typically produces no negative side effects. This is particularly true when occurrences of the target behavior are either ignored or feedback about it is given *very* matter-of-factly. (When responses are negative some of the same side effects that occur with punishment are seen; such as counteraggression and withdrawal from or avoidance of the situation.) Note, however, that the use of the reset variation of DRO often establishes reinforcement delivery as an S^D for problem behavior. This usually can be avoided by using the fixed-interval variation.
3. *Generalization of effects:* Preliminary research findings have suggested that DRO may contribute more to the generalization of treatment gains across settings than certain other intervention strategies.
4. *Speed of effects and social validity:* DRO has been shown to result in

rapid reduction of behavior problems. Further, and perhaps most important, it is socially acceptable to most staff. It is not complex to administer, nor does it draw negative attention to the learner, the staff, or the program.

There are several cautions that should be noted when using DRO to reduce problem behaviors. These include the following:

1. *Nonspecificity of response:* In the DRO procedure, no specifically identified response is reinforced. As long as the target response does not occur during the specified interval, reinforcement is presented. A problem may occur if the learner does not already have a rich and varied repertoire of functional behaviors (see chapter 1). The procedure could result in inactivity or the development of another problem. An example is shown in Figure 6.10. Again, it is important that DRO always be used in the context of a comprehensive instructional program.
2. *Inadvertent reinforcement:* Using DRO, we may unknowingly reinforce *any other* behavior. This may mean that a nontargeted, undesirable response is reinforced. Strategies for dealing with this were discussed earlier under suggestions for implementation.

FIGURE 6.10.   DRO procedures must be used in the context of positive programming

3. *Response occurrence after reinforcer delivery:* Another caution concerns the fact that delivery of a reinforcer can become a cue for the target behavior. This may be particularly true with a DRO reset schedule, where, for example, the reinforcer is a glass of juice given to a student who remains quiet for 1 hour, at which point the timer is reset. Since the timer is also reset whenever the student talks out, she may come to believe that it is necessary for her to talk out right after receiving juice in order to have the timer reset and get another chance to earn a glass of juice.

Another solution to the problem of response after reinforcement may be a DRO progressive (DROP) schedule of reinforcement for each consecutive interval in which the target behavior does not occur. Such progressive schedules eliminate the possibility of the learner maintaining the optimum density of reinforcement without sharply decreasing the frequency of responding, so they may therefore avoid the discriminative properties of reinforcement delivery for target responding.

7

Differential Reinforcement of Low Rates of Responding

Differential reinforcement of low rates of responding (DRL) involves either reinforcement after a response that follows an interval of specific length (DRL-IRT) or reinforcement after a specified interval, if the response rate is below some established criterion.

DRL is most effectively used to reduce high-rate behaviors. In some cases the behavior may be one that needs to be eliminated but the rate is so high that a DRO schedule would be difficult, as in the following example:

- Mary had 45 incidents of "abusive language" per workday. A DRO schedule required too many reinforcement intervals for a job coach to manage. A DRL procedure was used to reinforce her each hour in which there were eight or fewer occurrences of the behavior. The criterion number of occurrences was gradually reduced until the rate was low enough for a DRO procedure to be feasible.

In many cases the DRL schedule is implemented when dealing with a behavior that is only a problem because it occurs at an unacceptably high rate. In such a case, one may want to reduce but not completely eliminate the target behavior, as in the following example:

- An adolescent was taught to sign when she wanted to go out for a drink; however, she asked for a drink an average of 30 times per school day. Her teacher used a DRL procedure to reduce her requests to an average of one or two per hour or an average of seven per school day.

VARIATIONS OF *DRL*

DRL-IRT Schedules. The first variation (DRL-IRT) is one in which the *response* is reinforced following a specified interval since the previous response. The interval is gradually increased. This interval of time be-

85

tween responses is termed interresponse time (IRT); thus, the procedure is called DRL-IRT. Here is an example of how a DRL-IRT works:

- John, a student with dual sensory impairments, made many requests for an aide's assistance; the rate of such requests ranged from 3 to 20 per hour and averaged 6 times per hour over a 5-hour school day. The teacher believed John could be more independent and wanted him to learn to ask for help less often. With a baseline of six times per hour for a 5-hour day, he calculated that the interresponse time (IRT) for this behavior was 10 minutes (60 min. ÷ 6 occurrences).

    With this information, the aide set up a procedure in which he gave John assistance and praise for good work, provided that he asked for help *only* after at least 10 minutes (the identified IRT) had elapsed since the last request. If he asked for help before 10 minutes had elapsed, the aide, in a matter-of-fact manner, redirected him to continue working. Gradually the length of the interval was increased until John's requests for help decreased to a more reasonable rate; that is, as the time (interval length) between responses increases, the number of responses decreases.

    Figure 7.1 shows how the sequence of reinforcement might look initially. The first occurrence of the target behavior was at 9:00. Eleven minutes passed before the next request for help; therefore, the student received reinforcement. The next request occurred at 9:22, 11 minutes after the last request, so, again, reinforcement was delivered. The next request, however, came 2 minutes later at 9:24, so no reinforcement was delivered. John was matter-of-factly directed to return to work. Since the next request came at 9:35 (more than a 10-minute interval), reinforcement was again delivered; and so forth.

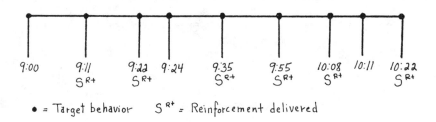

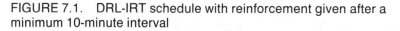

FIGURE 7.1.   DRL-IRT schedule with reinforcement given after a minimum 10-minute interval

DRL-Below-Criterion Schedules.   This variation of DRL involves determining the average number of times the target behavior is typically exhibited during a certain interval of time. Reinforcement is delivered if the frequency of the behavior is *below* this baseline rate during the specified interval of time, thus reinforcing lower rates of responding.

This procedure is different from DRL-IRT in that reinforcement occurs for each interval of time (e.g., every hour on the hour or at the end of each activity) during which the target behavior occurs at a lower rate — say, six or fewer times for the hour. Changing criteria are used to continue to reduce the target behavior. Here the interval is preset and it is the number of responses per interval that determines if the criterion for reinforcement is met. For example:

- David knocked materials off the table four times every hour. A procedure was designed so that reinforcement was delivered for every hour in which the behavior occurred less than four times. Figure 7.2 illustrates a possible sequence for this schedule. The behavior occurred only three times between 9:00 and 10:00 and three times between 10:00 and 11:00; in both intervals the rate was below baseline, and David therefore received reinforcement at 10:00 and 11:00. Between 11:00 and 12:00, however, the behavior occurred four times (the baseline rate), so at 12:00 no reinforcement was delivered. Between 12:00 and 1:00, the behavior occurred only twice, so reinforcement was again delivered at 1:00.

Additional target behaviors for which this variation of DRL has been used successfully are being "out-of-seat," talking out of turn, aggression, subject change in conversation (e.g., from academic subject to another, usually social, topic), and laughing. Note that the topographies of these behaviors are very different. While some would still be a problem even if they occurred at a low rate (aggression, for example), most were problems only because of their high frequency.

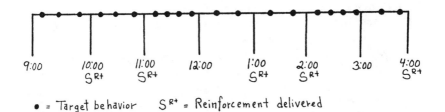

• = Target behavior   S R+ = Reinforcement delivered

FIGURE 7.2.   DRL-below-criterion schedule, with reinforcement given for response rate of fewer than four times per hour

SUGGESTIONS FOR IMPLEMENTING *DRL*

There are several important factors to be considered when implementing a DRL procedure:

1. Response rate
2. Learner ability and tangible monitoring system
3. Interval size and reinforcement criteria
4. Changing criteria
5. Reinforcement magnitude

Response Rate.   As discussed, DRL is most effectively used to reduce high-rate behaviors, and it is used often when dealing with a behavior that is only a problem because it occurs at an unacceptably high rate. To determine if this is the case, before beginning, collect data, make sure you have a stable baseline, and compare the baseline to what can be expected from nonhandicapped peers and/or what is considered an acceptable occurrence rate of the behavior in the natural environment.

Learner Ability and Tangible Monitoring Systems.   Remember, it is not necessary that learners be able to understand an explanation of the procedure in order for it to be effective. If learner abilities are limited, the effectiveness of the procedure can be enhanced by using concrete, tangible feedback systems. As an example, individuals with dual sensory impairments may be helped by and enjoy tracking their performance using pleasing tactile feedback systems, such as moving marbles from one container to the next, switching tickets from one pocket to the other, and the like. Other feedback systems that can be used, depending on individual ability, include signs or pictures of the reinforcer that can be moved or turned to the wall, tokens moved from pocket to pocket, checkmarks, "lite-brite" displays, and so forth.

Some critical aspects to consider when using tangible feedback are:

1. Movement of the markers or other items is *not* meant to be aversive. Directions to move the item should be given in a very matter-of-fact manner and with no emotional overlay.
2. Markers or other items are *moved*, *not* taken away. If they are removed, the procedure becomes response cost, which is aversive.
3. Reinforcement is not tied to the number of markers or other items that are left. The same reinforcer (in the same amount) is given as long as *any* markers are left at the end of an interval.

Interval Size and Reinforcement Criteria.   The rate of behavior and not the interval size is critical to implementing a DRL schedule. The interval, therefore, can correspond to the time frame of natural events, and the acceptable level of the behavior can be increased or decreased proportionally. The effectiveness of the strategy depends on the reinforcement criterion rather than the size of the time interval. We recommend using the baseline rate of the behavior as the *initial* criterion for reinforcement. Consider the following example:

- Anne threw things an average of 12 times during a 6-hour school day. Four DRL intervals were established to coincide with a typical day's schedule: the 2-hour interval from the start of the day through snack time, the 1-hour period for community instruction, the 1½-hour interval that ended right after lunch, and the vocational training activity for the last 1½-hour period of the day. The criteria for reinforcement for these four intervals were as follows: first interval (8:30–10:30), no more than four throws for reinforcement; second interval (10:30–11:30), no more than two throws for reinforcement; third interval (11:30–1:00), no more than three throws for reinforcement; and fourth interval (1:00–2:30), no more than three throws for reinforcement.

Changing Criteria.   The criterion for reinforcement should be lowered only after a new steady state has been reached and maintained for an acceptable amount of time. For example, Figure 7.3 shows how a changing criterion was used to lower the rate of Roy's tendency to engage in provocative verbal confrontations. His teacher calculated that these occurred about 25 times each school day. She set the criterion at 23 confrontations per day and gradually reduced the criterion to more acceptable levels. A steady state of 5 days at criterion was used as a decision rule for lowering criterion.

Reinforcement Magnitude.   It is important to remember the free access rule (see chapter 6) when using a DRL schedule:

- George earned cans of soda as reinforcement. It was important to note how many cans of soda he drank when he had free access. He would ordinarily drink three in a school day, if allowed. Therefore, a can each hour would have been too much. Instead, he was reinforced with a small glass of soda. Soon the teacher extended the DRL interval so that the total earnable cans of soda was significantly less than three per school day.

ADVANTAGES OF USING *DRL*

There are several important advantages that DRL strategies can contribute to reducing behavior problems. These include

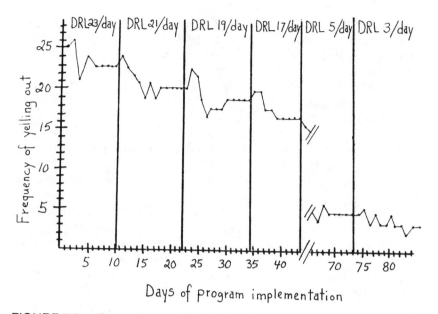

FIGURE 7.3.   Example of a DRL reinforcement schedule with changing criterion designed to lower rate of responding gradually

1. *Reduction of High-Rate Behavior:* As mentioned, DRL procedures can be very useful when the problem behavior occurs at such high rates that a DRO procedure is unfeasible, or when the behavior is only a problem because of its high rate. For example, a behavior that occurred 10 times per hour was reduced to 2 or 3 times per hour using a DRL. The behavior, aggression, was serious even at low rates; therefore, a DRO 15-minute procedure was then used to eliminate the behavior (see Figure 7.4).

   Behaviors that are not serious at reasonable rates, such as stereotypic behaviors or repetitive questions, could be maintained at the minimum level achievable using DRL, without further intervention. A guide for establishing a reasonable rate can be found in the natural environment by observing the learner's peers. Such observation will help determine what is normal for other learners in particular environments. For example:
   - Being off task at work was a problem for Mike. He frequently stopped to talk to other workers. To determine how much this behavior needed to be reduced, Mike's job coach observed Mike's fellow workers to determine how much off-task time and talking was typical. That was then considered the reasonable rate.

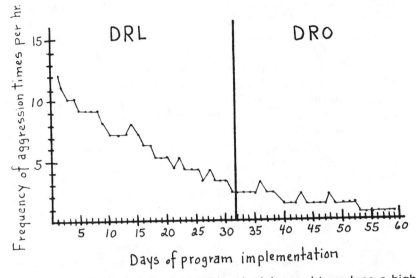

FIGURE 7.4. Effective use of a DRL schedule used to reduce a high rate of aggression, with a DRO schedule used to eliminate it entirely

2. *Flexible Intervals:* Another advantage when using a DRL strategy is that you can set the time interval size at virtually any length, fitting the flow of events in the natural setting. The time interval can vary across sessions, activities, and settings. This flexibility is possible because the critical aspect of the procedure is not the *size* of the interval, but the *rate* of occurrence of the target behavior during the period. The following is a case in point:
   - Jeanne laughed inappropriately on her job site at an average rate of 8 times per hour. The DRL interval could have been 30 minutes or 1 hour, or it could have been made to correspond with natural break times. The interval of 2.5 hours fit nicely with arrival, coffee break, lunch, midday, and quitting time. Jeanne received reinforcement at those times if she had not laughed inappropriately more than 19 times during the preceding interval. The criterion for reinforcement was gradually reduced over time. Using natural break times minimized disruption on the work site and allowed the use of reinforcements that might otherwise have been stigmatizing (such as food or extra time with a favorite supervisor).
3. *Variable Reinforcement Selection:* The flexible DRL interval offers the advantage of varying the total amount of reinforcement, as well as the

kind of reinforcement available, so that the individual is less likely to satiate on the reinforcer. A student might get a can of soda at break at his work site and an extra 10-minute game period in the classroom. Again, remember the issue of free access when determining the appropriate amount of the various reinforcers to be used.

4. *Tangible Feedback:* Comments in the literature and our experience suggest that the success of DRL procedures is enhanced by using concrete, tangible feedback systems to help impaired students understand the rules and keep track of their behavior. DRL lends itself particularly well to such systems because the learners can actually see the criterion change as their behavior changes.

5. *Speed of Effects:* DRL schedules can lead to rapid control of the target behavior. In spite of this, staff sometimes become concerned when learners consistently perform the behavior at the maximum allowable level that they can and still receive reinforcement.

   • Ethan received reinforcement if he left his seat less than six times per hour. For awhile he got out of his seat exactly five times each hour. His teacher was concerned that he was "having his cake and eating it, too." In fact, this situation should have been viewed as encouraging, as it indicated that he clearly understood the contingency. This being the case, control can be established even more rapidly.

6. *Potential for Group Contingencies:* DRL schedules also offer the advantage of using one intervention to modify the behavior of an entire group in a classroom or other setting. This provides ease of management and efficient use of staff time. One requirement in this situation is the identification of a reinforcer that would be comparably effective for all members of a group. If this requirement cannot be met by a single primary reinforcer, a token system can be used whereby each learner can cash in tokens for individualized reinforcers. The following is an example of a group DRL program:

   • The target behavior was obscene words or gestures. The class of six boys and three girls received half an hour of free time during the last part of the day, on any day that less than 16 obscene words or gestures, directed toward each other or school staff, were used. For example, on one particular day, from 9:00 to 10:00 the target behavior occurred twice, so two checks were entered on the scoreboard (see Figure 7.5) for the first hour. The behavior occurred three times from 10:00 to 11:00, so three checks were entered, and so on. By the end of the day, at 3:30, the class had been successful in keeping the frequency of the target behavior below 16, so they received half an hour of free time that day.

Scoreboard

Time	9–10	10–11	11–12	12–1	1–2	2–3	
Words	✓✓	✓✓✓	✓	✓	✓✓✓	✓	11
Gestures			✓✓	✓	✓		4 = 15

FIGURE 7.5.   Class scoreboard for group DRL program to reduce obscene words and gestures

7. *Nonspecific Reinforcement:* A final advantage of the DRL schedule is that the reinforcer maintaining the target behavior does not need to be identified, as long as the reinforcer used in the DRL schedule can compete successfully with it. If the consequence for engaging in behavior at a decreased rate is more powerful than the consequence for maintaining the behavior at higher rates, the behavior should be weakened and begin to occur less often. In the case just discussed, for example, the teacher may not have known exactly what was maintaining the use of obscenities. She had, however, analyzed previous behavior of the class and determined that free time would reinforce the lower rate of behavior and that the social pressure of making it a group contingency added to its effectiveness. The data indicate she was correct. After 2 weeks she lowered the criterion to 14 or fewer responses per day and continued to reduce it every 2 weeks thereafter, until reaching a more acceptable level (4 per day).

CAUTIONS IN USING *DRL*

There are a number of cautions that should be considered when using a DRL schedule to reduce behavior problems. These include the following:

1. *The non-constructive nature of the procedure:* One problem with using DRL procedures, as with DROs, is that they do not teach appropriate alternative behaviors. Reducing the use of obscenities, as in the previous example, may certainly be important. However, giving the students less socially offensive strategies for expressing anger, particularly toward authority figures, is also important. Moreover, a rich and varied curriculum will give learners opportunities to engage in many other behaviors for which they can be reinforced.

2. *Concerns regarding social validity:* When using DRL schedules, another concern is social validity. Some staff find it difficult to reinforce a

learner (or group of learners) who have engaged in inappropriate behaviors. It is important to remember that the ultimate goal is to *reduce* the behavior and that reinforcement on a DRL schedule may be an essential step.

A related issue, as mentioned earlier, is that some persons feel that the learner is being "manipulative" if she figures out the schedule and then does one less than the criterion number. While this may be a bit annoying at first, it can be seen as the first step in creating an overall pattern of reduction of the behavior. This is demonstrated in Figure 7.6, which shows how the behavior gradually comes under the control of the schedule of reinforcement and is reduced in frequency as the criteria are reduced. Rather than complaining when the learner "slips in under the wire," these kind of data are cause for celebration!

3. *Potential for an aversive component:* Another concern is that the information feedback mechanism used in conjunction with the DRL schedule may bring a mildly aversive quality to the intervention. A monitoring system must be designed only to keep learners informed of their responses and to minimize the aversive potential. For example, when moving the marble, taking the ticket, or otherwise indicating that the target behavior has occurred, it is best to have the student keep track herself, if possible. And, as previously mentioned, whether the student or teacher keeps track, the monitoring should be kept nonaversive. The teacher could say, for example, "Well, you shouted out — turn the picture to the wall." And if the student fails to meet the criterion, the teacher can say, in a matter-of-fact manner, "Looks like you missed out this time. Better luck this afternoon" or, "You'll have another chance tomorrow."

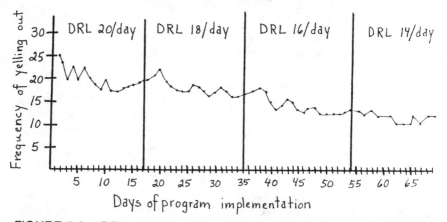

FIGURE 7.6.   DRL data showing a typical pattern of gradual behavior reduction

8

Differential Reinforcement of Alternative Behaviors

Differential reinforcement of alternative behaviors (DRA) involves the selective reinforcement of those behaviors that are topographically different from the target behavior. This procedure also is called the differential reinforcement of incompatible behaviors (DRI) and the differential reinforcement of competing behaviors (DRC). We will refer to it here, however, as Alt-R. Examples of topographically different behavior pairs include biting one's fingernails versus knitting; running around the classroom versus sitting at one's desk; and grabbing items off the store shelf versus walking the aisles while pushing a cart with both hands.

ESSENTIAL CONSIDERATIONS IN THE USE OF *Alt-R*

The literature indicates there are a variety of ways that Alt-R has been used. We believe that inadequate attention to the manipulation of several essential variables has resulted in some confusion about the effectiveness of Alt-R. These variables are:

1. Absence of motor behavior as the identified alternative response
2. Topographical similarity versus dissimilarity
3. Topographical compatibility versus incompatibility
4. The 100% rule
5. Scheduling of reinforcement and intervention
6. Preintervention status of the alternative response
7. Reinforcement identification and specification

The Absence of Motor Behavior as the Identified Alternative Response. Problems in using the Alt-R procedure may occur when the

95

alternative response is defined as nonbehavior. Instead, the task is to vary and increase behavioral repertoires, in order to make them more functional. Moreover, if persons with problem behaviors simply stopped responding, we would end up with a noninteracting, immobile person, which is clearly *not* the goal of education or treatment. Not only is such an approach detrimental to the learner, it is also unfair, especially when the learner has only a limited performance repertoire. For a behavior such as stereotypic rocking, for example, the alternative response may be defined as "sitting still," but this alternative is in fact a nonbehavior that is actually physiologically impossible, as there is a minimum level of motor response present in all human beings. Appropriate alternative behaviors to stereotypic rocking might include dancing to music, rocking in a chair, or walking with a normal gait. The alternative behavior that is reinforced should be something the person needs to do or at least might enjoy doing, a criterion all three of these responses meet.

Topographical Similarity Versus Dissimilarity.   A second consideration of Alt-R concerns how similar the alternative response is to the target behavior. The more physically different the target behavior and the alternative response, the better, particularly if the learner has trouble with fine discriminations. Examples of topographically similar and dissimilar alternatives for several behaviors are given in Table 8.1.

TABLE 8.1.   Topographically similar and dissimilar alternative responses to target behaviors

Target Behavior	Alternative Responses	
	Topographically Similar	Topographically Dissimilar
Hands in mouth	Tooth brushing	Doing needlepoint
Hitting others	Touching others softly	Waving or tipping one's hat to others
Head banging	Combing hair	Typing
Spitting on others	Spitting into a kleenex	Chewing gum
Throwing materials	Playing basketball	Writing a story

Topographical Compatibility Versus Incompatibility.   A third consid-. eration of Alt-R involves topographical compatibility or incompatibility of the alternative behaviors with the target behavior. For example, if the target behavior is self-hitting, a topographically *compatible* alternative response is singing. That is, although unlikely, it is physically possible to sing and hit oneself at the same time. Having both hands in one's pockets is an example of behavior that is topographically *incompatible* with the target behavior of self-hitting. The general rule is to choose alternative responses that are as incompatible with the target behavior as possible, obviously increasing the effectiveness of this strategy. Some other examples of compatible and incompatible alternative behaviors are given in Table 8.2.

Satisfying the 100% Rule.   Some studies have shown that, even when the alternative response is topographically dissimilar and incompatible, the target behavior may not be reduced. In such cases, application of the "100% rule" may not have occurred. This rule requires defining the target behavior and the alternative response so that together they cover the universe of possible alternative behaviors. That is, *by definition*, the learner is either engaging in the target behavior or in the alternative response, with no third option possible. For example, if the targeted behavior is getting out of one's seat, then an alternative response that satisfies the 100% rule would be staying in one's seat. One cannot be in one's seat and out of it at the same time; there is no third option possible. Thus, if we reinforce a learner for being in her seat and increase this behavior over baseline levels, we will inevitably be decreasing the amount of time she spends out of her seat.

Problems occur when the target behavior and the alternative response have not been *defined* such that they represent the universe of possibilities. When this happens, it may be possible to increase the alternative response without decreasing the target behavior. For example, if out-of-seat behavior occurs 10% of the time and writing occurs 20% of the time, we could reinforce and increase writing behavior significantly and not necessarily reduce out-of-seat behavior. Writing thus is an alternative response that does not satisfy the 100% rule in this instance. Table 8.3 gives a few more applications of this rule.

There are complex application issues regarding the 100% rule which have been inadequately addressed, even by many researchers who have investigated Alt-R procedures. This may explain at least partially the mixed results in the Alt-R literature. We think it is particularly important to highlight these issues because Alt-R is often the only positive procedure

TABLE 8.2. Topographically compatible and incompatible alternative responses to target behaviors

Target Behavior	Alternative Responses	
	Topographically Compatible	Topographically Incompatible
Nail biting	Handwriting	Knitting
Hand flapping	Keeping arms at one's side	Hands in pockets; carying things in both hands
Screaming	Listening to music	Playing a wind instrument
Feces smearing	Watching television	Playing a hand held video game

attempted by teachers, staff, and researchers before a punishment procedure is used. Given the problems in meeting the 100% rule, we may want to reconsider the practice of Alt-R and use it only under limited conditions.

The following guidelines are presented to assist you in implementing an Alt-R procedure. Difficulty in applying these guidelines may lead to a decision to use some of the other nonaversive techniques discussed in this book.

Some behaviors are naturally of an either/or nature and easily meet the 100% rule. Being in one place or not, being on time or not, doing what one has been asked to do or not, and completing one's assignment or not all exemplify such behaviors. In order to use the Alt-R procedure, you must be able to define a specific alternative behavior to be reinforced; that is, you cannot simply reinforce the absence of a certain response, as in a DRO procedure.

It may help to clarify the 100% rule if we review DRO and DRL within the present context. In their own way, DRO and DRL satisfy the 100% rule. With DRO, the universe of possibilities is defined as the occurrence or nonoccurrence of the *target behavior* during specified intervals of time. For example, if the target behavior is aggression, we can determine that, for each time interval, aggression either occurs or does not occur. Therefore, if we reinforce and successfully increase the number of intervals that are free of aggression, we will by definition be decreasing the number of intervals that include aggression (see Figure 8.1).

DRL has a similar feature. In this case, the universe of possibilities is defined as the occurrence of the target behavior above, at, or below some

TABLE 8.3. Examples of application of the 100% rule

Target Behavior	Alternative Response	100% Rule Satisfied?	Explanation
Talking out	Answering Questions	No	A Person may talk out, answer questions, ask questions after politely interrupting and getting someone's attention, read, write, or engage in any number of other responses. Increasing the answering of questions will not necessarily reduce the amount of talking out a person does.
Running	Walking	No	A person may run, skip, jump, sit, swim, and so forth. Increasing walking will not necessarily reduce running.
Being late for class	Being on time for class	Yes	A person is expected to come to class a fixed number of times. He can either be late or on time. (A no-show would be defined as the ultimate lateness.) Increasing the number of times a person is on time will, by definition, decrease the number of times he is late.
Not doing what someone asks (noncompliance)	Doing what someone asks (compliance)	Yes	A person can either do what is asked or not. If we increase the rate of compliance, by definition we will decrease the rate of noncompliance.

specified criterion during specified intervals of time. For example, if the target behavior is talking out of turn, we can determine that, for each interval, this behavior either occurs more than five times or occurs five times or less. Therefore, if we reinforce and successfully increase the number of intervals that have five or fewer incidents of talking out of turn, we will automatically decrease the number of intervals that have more than five occurrences (see Figure 8.2).

As we discussed, it may be possible to satisfy the 100% rule with the Alt-R procedure with certain behaviors, such as compliance versus noncompliance or in-seat versus out-of-seat behavior. In such cases increasing one behavior will, by necessity, result in the decrease of the other. Increasing the rate of compliance will result in a decrease in the rate of noncompliance and increasing the rate of in-seat behavior will result in a decrease of out-of-seat behavior (see Figure 8.3).

Such a decrease may not occur, however, if we cannot define the behaviors to satisfy the 100% rule. For example, if we want to decrease aggression and attempt to do so by increasing the alternative response of appropriate play and/or the alternative response of completing academic assignments, the situation would look like that in Figure 8.4. Upon implementation of our Alt-R strategy, we may very well increase the rate of academic work and appropriate play; however, as shown in Figure 8.4, B, this will not necessarily result in a decrease in the rate of aggression.

Where we cannot satisfy the 100% rule, we may effectively decrease the target behavior by increasing the number of alternative responses we target for reinforcement, in order to approximate the 100% rule. In such cases, we would want to combine the Alt-R with the separate application of DRO, DRL, or some other alternative strategy also aimed at decreasing the problem behavior, in order to assure success.

To summarize, while it is imperative to meet the 100% rule to insure the success of an Alt-R procedure, in practice it is very difficult to do so. When it is not possible to meet the 100% rule, you may have to add another procedure to insure a decrease in the undesired behavior. For example, a given learner may not be able to do math work and talk to a neighbor simultaneously. If, however, the target behavior is her talking to neighbors, we will more likely be effective in reducing it if we not only reinforce and increase her math productivity (Alt-R) but also reinforce her for specified intervals that are free of talking to her neighbors (DRO). The two combined may prove more effective than either one alone (see Figure 8.5).

Scheduling of Reinforcement and Intervention.   As with any procedure, once we have determined what we intend to reinforce, we must determine the schedule of reinforcement to use. In applying an Alt-R

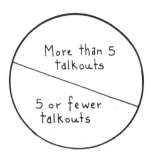

FIGURE 8.1. Example of a DRO schedule as it meets the 100% rule

FIGURE 8.2. Example of a DRL schedule with a criterion of 5 as it meets the 100% rule

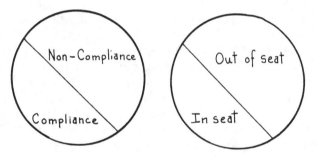

FIGURE 8.3. Example of behaviors that by definition meet the 100% rule

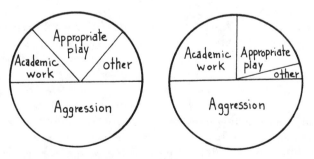

FIGURE 8.4. Possible redistribution of behavior resulting from an Alt-R strategy that fails to meet the 100% rule

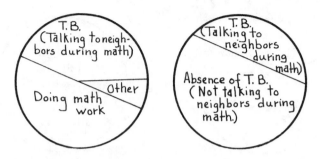

FIGURE 8.5. Combining Alt-R and DRO when alternate behavior cannot be defined to meet the 100% rule

procedure, even if we successfully meet the 100% rule we still may have difficulty in specifying the reinforcement schedule. Let's consider the example of in-seat versus out-of-seat behavior. No teacher could realistically believe that she could reinforce in-seat behavior continuously. In fact, in a group situation, it would be nearly impossible even to monitor the behaviors without the use of complex mechanical devices that allow for continuous recording. Clearly, one must specify some other means of determining when to reinforce. Instead, the teacher might decide to reinforce the student for every 5 consecutive minutes she spends in her seat. Or, the teacher may decide to sample the behavior once every 5 minutes: If the student is in her seat, she receives reinforcement; if not, she does not. Remember, the choice of intervention will determine how data are collected (see chapter 5).

In addition to working out a reinforcement schedule, we must also decide on a schedule for the intervention itself. It may not always be possible — or desirable — to apply an Alt-R procedure over 24 hours or even throughout an entire school day. Instead, staff may want to specify certain times when the intervention is in effect. If, for example, you want to increase compliance or speaking in complete sentences, you have to realize that it may not be practical to provide a consequence for every successful occasion. Rather, you may address only a specified list of requests and provide reinforcement when the learner complies for these occasions only. Because of other pragmatic issues, you may want to limit further application of the intervention by specifying particular periods of the day during which the intervention will be in place. For example, you only may record and reinforce a learner for asking for permission from 9 to 10 A.M. and from 1 to 2 P.M. This kind of time limiting may be more practical in many situations.

Preintervention Status of the Alternative Response.   Another consideration in the use of Alt-R concerns the presence of the alternative response in the learner's repertoire prior to the intervention. The alternative response must already exist to some extent in the learner's repertoire during the baseline condition. If the behavior does not occur, obviously it cannot be reinforced. In such cases, it is not possible to apply an Alt-R procedure alone. Rather, the Alt-R strategy should be combined with prompt and prompt-fading or some other instructional technique, in order to assure the development and occurrence of the alternative response (see chapters 3 and 10). In some cases such instruction may be required for some time before the Alt-R procedure can be implemented.

The following examples illustrate our points on this matter:

- Barbara was often, but not always, late for math class. Her teacher set up a program in which every time Barbara arrived early or on time she was allowed to go down to the principal's office and run errands for the secretary (one of her favorite things to do).
- Darryl *never* hung his coat up when he came in but simply dropped it on the floor. In this case, simply reinforcing Darryl for hanging up his coat would not be effective in reducing the number of times he dropped it on the floor, since he never hung up his coat. Therefore, staff combined Alt-R with a prompt/prompt-fading strategy and were effective in their intervention efforts.

Reinforcement Identification and Specification

Another strategy in Alt-R uses an already occurring consequence and simply rearranges the relationship between that consequence and the learner's behavior in the natural setting. This is done in an effort to increase desired responses and decrease undesired ones. For example, if it was hypothesized that the target behavior was being maintained by adult attention, then by systematically paying attention to an alternative response and ignoring the behavior targeted for reduction, the alternative response could be effectively reinforced.

- *Teacher to class*: "I know you used to be able to get my attention by talking out and calling my name. From now on I will only answer a student who raises his or her hand and waits quietly to be called on."
- *Mother to child*: "I used to nag at you whenever you left your

clothes lying around your room. From now on I will spend extra time playing a game with you when you put your clothes in the new hamper."

SUGGESTIONS FOR IMPLEMENTING *Alt-R*

Following are suggestions for implementation that should help to make Alt-R a more effective strategy for reducing behavior problems.

Choose Topographically Different and Incompatible Responses. In order to assure the effectiveness of the Alt-R procedure, an alternative response should be selected that is as physically different from the target behavior as possible. In addition, it should be incompatible with the target behavior; that is, it should be physically impossible for the two to occur simultaneously.

Apply the 100% Rule. Whenever possible, the target behavior and the identified alternative response should be defined in such a way as to represent the universe of possibilities. In this way, by necessity, an increase in the alternative response guarantees a decrease in the target behavior. If one satisfies the 100% rule, the need for a different and incompatible topography for the alternative response is already met.

Select Multiple Responses. Meeting the 100% rule is difficult. If it cannot be met, then several alternative responses should be identified for reinforcement. With the addition of each incompatible response, the 100% rule can be more closely approximated and at least satisfied empirically, if not by definition. For example, if the target behavior is cursing, then making positive comments, reading quietly, and listening to music might be an effective combination of alternative responses. If hitting others on the playground is the target behavior, an appropriate alternative response combination might include riding the merry-go-round, swinging, playing chase, and climbing.

Choose a Presently Occurring Behavior. We recommend that the alternative response already be in the learner's repertoire and be occurring at some level. If an existing response is not selected, training and other preliminary procedures (e.g., prompting) may be necessary.

Select a Reinforcer for the Alternative Response. If possible, the reinforcer used to strengthen the alternative response should be the one that was previously maintaining the target behavior, and Alt-R should be used in combination with extinction of the behavior to be reduced. Contrived reinforcers are less desirable than naturally occurring ones, as reinforcement may need to continue indefinitely. It is also a good idea to "thin" the reinforcement schedule gradually, in order to make the alternative response resistant to extinction. For example:

- Ms. Jones was trying to decrease the time James spent out of his seat by reinforcing him with check marks for being in his seat. He earned one check mark for every 5 consecutive minutes he spent in his seat. He turned in his marks for various items on his reinforcement menu. Ms. Jones planned to increase gradually the number of minutes James stayed in his seat for a check mark.

Consider Using Mediating Systems.   It is sometimes effective, once you have identified a list of alternative responses to be reinforced, to use a mediating system such as a token economy. In this case the learner could receive tokens as reinforcement following the occurrence of each of the several identified alternative behaviors. These tokens would, in turn, be exchangeable for items such as privileges, awards, food, free time, and so on. Once the behavioral objectives have been accomplished, the artificial token system should be gradually faded and control shifted to a more direct delivery of natural consequences.

When determining the amount of reinforcer to offer, take the free access rule into account, making sure the learner is only able to earn about 60% of the amount of reinforcer he would ordinarily seek.

Use Appropriate Schedules of Reinforcement.   Alternative responses can be defined in terms of frequency and/or duration. When alternative responses have been defined in terms of discrete frequencies, a continuous reinforcement (CRF) schedule initially would be used. Once the alternative responses are stable, the schedule would gradually be thinned to a fixed-ratio (FR), variable-ratio (VR), and ultimately you might change to a variable-interval (VI) format (see chapter 2). Figure 8.6 shows the use of increasingly thinner schedules of reinforcement. Fixed and variable schedules can also be applied to behaviors that have been defined in terms of duration. Increasing interval size produces increasingly thinner schedules of reinforcement and makes alternative responses more resistant to extinction.

Use Alt-R with Other Procedures.   Our final recommendation is that Alt-R be used in combination with other procedures. This will enhance its effectiveness and contribute to the possibility of long-term treatment ef-

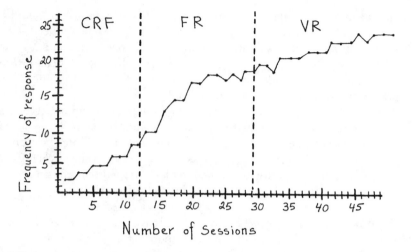

FIGURE 8.6.   Increasing the frequency of alternative responses via use of increasingly thinner schedules of reinforcement

fects. Specifically, we recommend the use of Alt-R with positive programming, differential reinforcement of other behavior (DRO), differential reinforcement of low rates of behavior (DRL), and extinction.

CONCLUSION

There are at least three advantages of Alt-R as a strategy for reducing undesired responding: lasting results, constructive approach, and social validity.

1. *Lasting results:* When reinforcing and increasing an alternative response results in the decrease of a target behavior, the reduction can be maintained over a long period of time. It may be necessary to continue reinforcement of the alternative response indefinitely. Certain sequences of reinforcement schedules, such as moving from a CRF to a VR schedule, make alternative responses more resistant to extinction and make the target behavior more resistant to recovery.
2. *Constructive approach:* One of the most appealing aspects of Alt-R as a strategy for reducing behavior problems is its constructive approach. Not only may the procedure eliminate or reduce undesired behavior,

but, in addition, Alt-R increases the frequency and overall production of desirable behavior in the learner's observed repertoire.

3. *Social validity:* Because of its constructive and positive approach, teachers, aides, parents, direct-care workers, consumer representatives, administrators, psychologists, and other professionals find Alt-R a comfortable and popular procedure to use.

The constructive nature of Alt-R justifies its prominent placement on any list of nonaversive intervention strategies. Its successful application requires consideration of the procedure's complexities. The cautions regarding the use of this procedure include delayed effect, complexity and mixed evidence of effectiveness, and recovery and rebound.

1. *Delayed effect:* One problem with Alt-R in reducing undesired responding is that the results may not occur immediately. In a situation where the target behavior is self-abuse, for example, any delay in treatment effects would be cause for concern. Therefore, if rapid control is urgently required, an alternative or at least an additional concurrent approach should be considered.

2. *Complexity and mixed evidence of effectiveness:* Because Alt-R is a complex procedure, it can be difficult to implement. Under many conditions, however, it is a highly effective strategy with a constructive approach, making it extremely valuable. It is likely that with careful thought and planning certain problems can be eliminated. To date, there is mixed evidence in the behavioral literature regarding the effectiveness of Alt-R. It is our opinion that unspecified, uncontrolled, and/or arbitrarily designated variables may, in part, explain the mixed reviews. The optimum design of the Alt-R procedure has yet to be defined. Many suggestions have been presented in this chapter for increasing its effectiveness.

3. *Recovery and rebound:* Undesired behavior that has been reduced or eliminated using an Alt-R strategy tends to recover to baseline levels when reinforcement for the alternative response is terminated. Several suggestions involving a shift to natural contingencies were presented previously in the implementation section. These should help address this recovery effect. Particular attention should be paid to these strategies, as failure to do so may result in higher rates of target behavior than were observed prior to the implementation strategy.

9

Stimulus Control

Stimulus control refers to the discriminative control of behavior. The underlying principle is that, in the presence of certain stimuli, a behavior is more likely to be reinforced and therefore is more likely to occur.

At an early age we learn that some behaviors are more appropriate in certain settings than others. Toileting, using foul language, and engaging in sexual intercourse are examples of behavior for which the setting cues are very clear in a given culture. Toileting occurs in the bathroom, foul language does *not* occur in church, and sexual intercourse is done in privacy. Some setting cues, however, are less clear. For example, when children first start school, they must learn the "rules," social and otherwise, some of which are more subtle and less consistent than others. In Mr. Ahren's classroom, students may be allowed to put their feet on their desks, while in Ms. Grundy's, feet must be on the floor. Both settings are similar, yet the students learn the "rules" fairly readily. Our behavior comes under the control of the setting, whether or not the original stimuli (in this case, the different teachers) are present or even explicitly identified.

Consider another example. Someone can tell the same joke in two settings, a church and a nightclub. It will not, however, produce the same reaction, even if the same people are in the audience. What does this mean for our staff, and how can we use this information to manage problem behavior?

We can use stimulus control to help manage a variety of behaviors. In some cases, the problem may be that the learner simply does not know the "rules." He engages in the "wrong" behavior at the "wrong" time or in the "wrong" place. By teaching him where and when it is all right to perform the behavior, we are using stimulus control. For example:

- Sam spent much of his study time talking to other students. The study hall teacher felt that this was a situation where the behavior was acceptable, but *not* in that setting. The teacher wanted to encourage the behavior (social interaction) under certain conditions (outside at recess).

108

At times, we may want certain stimuli to set the occasion for the occurrence of a specific behavior or set of behaviors to be reinforced. This is particularly important for teaching independence in the natural environment, when we want certain behaviors to occur only in response to certain stimuli. If these stimuli signal the availability of reinforcement for certain behaviors, the behaviors are more likely to occur. For example, when the recess bell rings, it sets the occasion (provides the stimulus) for students to line up and go outside to be able to play. When the bus arrives, it sets the occasion (provides the stimulus) for the opportunity to ride the bus. Consider also the following case:

- Jeff made odd noises that drew attention at his job-training site. His job trainer reinforced him for such noises when he was wearing a certain hat. He was not allowed to wear the hat at work, and soon no longer made the noises there. Now he only makes the noises when he wears the hat during free time.

DISCRIMINATIVE STIMULI

In what way do stimuli establish control over behaviors and indicate the availability of reinforcement for those behaviors? The answer lies in the reinforcement history of the behaviors. If certain behaviors are under stimulus control, it means that in the past they have been reinforced in the presence of those stimuli and *not* reinforced when those same stimuli were absent. For example, asking directions of another person is likely to be reinforced with information enabling you to get to your destination; asking questions when there is nobody to answer will obviously not result in helpful information. Similarly, ordering a soda will likely be reinforced with receiving one when a waiter is present; when he is not present, the same behavior will not be reinforced.

The stimuli that set the occasion for the behavior are called *discriminative stimuli* (S^D). They indicate that, should the behavior occur, reinforcement is available. So, in the example of ordering a soda, the presence of the waiter in the restaurant is the discriminative stimulus.

On the other hand, the absence of the S^D (when the waiter is not there) is referred to as the S^Δ (S-delta) condition. The S^Δ condition indicates that, even if the behavior occurs, it will not be reinforced.

Thus, stimulus control is established to the extent that future occurrences of a given behavior (e.g., asking for a soda) happen under the S^D condition (waiter available) and tend not to happen under the S^Δ condition (waiter not available).

An important point to consider when deciding to use a stimulus-control procedure is the frequency of the response (target behavior). This procedure is highly recommended when the issue becomes one of bringing a behavior under more acceptable stimulus control. It is not recommended when the absolute frequency of a response is the critical issue. For example, most persons would agree that masturbation in private is an acceptable behavior. Masturbation in public, however, is unacceptable. Thus, if masturbation were reinforced under specific private conditions, it would likely be under more acceptable stimulus control. Consider this case example:

- The problem behavior was students talking to each other in class. Here the problem behavior was not one the English teacher wanted to eliminate completely; rather, he wanted it to occur only under certain conditions or at certain times. One option he had was to establish a sharing time, during which students were actually given additional reinforcers for talking with each other. He made the times even more clear to the students by having a sign go up when it was an acceptable time to talk. Over time, the talking came under the control of the "sharing-time" sign.

SUGGESTIONS FOR IMPLEMENTING STIMULUS CONTROL

There are at least three considerations in applying stimulus-control procedures successfully: the choice of target behavior, the selection of a reinforcer, and the selection of a discriminative stimulus.

Choosing the Target Behavior.   Behaviors such as stereotypic motor responses, undesired verbalizations, and inappropriate sexual behaviors respond well to stimulus-control interventions. One rule of thumb is to avoid using stimulus control with ultimately dangerous behaviors (e.g., physical aggression, self-injury, or property destruction), because these are behaviors we would want to eliminate and/or reshape completely.

In addition, when considering stimulus control as a behavior management strategy for a particular response, you already should have an ultimate goal in mind. For example, if your goal is to bring the behavior under more limited stimulus conditions, to reduce its frequency and, if possible, to eliminate it, there are important implications for the eventual identification and specification of the S^D. Also, you want to make sure you have complete control of the S^D. For example, in the case discussed earlier, where a young man learned to make noises only when he was wearing his special hat, the hat was chosen as the S^D for two reasons. First, its accessibility was controlled by the job trainer. Second, an ultimate goal was for the young man to control his own behavior in a nonstigmatizing way. Few people would suspect he was practicing self-control by wearing a special hat at certain times.

Selecting a Reinforcer.   Some reinforcers are intrinsic to (or part of) a response, some are extrinsic to (not part of) a response, and some are both. The range of possibilities can be seen in the case of aggression. On the one hand, aggressive action may in itself bring about a decrease in a learner's physical tension, thus providing intrinsic reinforcement — that is, reinforcement that results solely from the response, without regard to anything external to the individual. On the other hand, a learner's aggressive behavior might cause those with whom he is interacting to accede to his demands, which would then be extrinsic reinforcement. Aggression is therefore a response susceptible to both intrinsic and extrinsic reinforcement. Consideration of a few more possible responses may help to demonstrate these distinctions: Talking to oneself, riding a bike, masturbation, hand flapping, playing solitaire, and making noises, for example, are all behaviors that may be intrinsically reinforcing; behaviors aimed at eliciting praise, money, attention, or tokens of any kind are subject to extrinsic reinforcement; and talking out, building something, and playing music are behaviors that may be both intrinsically and extrinsically reinforced.

It is important to identify which reinforcers are maintaining the behavior. If the behavior (such as hand flapping) is intrinsically maintained, a more powerful extrinsic reinforcer (perhaps an opportunity to engage in social interaction with a favorite person) may be used in the presence of an S^D such as a special chair to help establish stimulus control over this response. Gradually the extrinsic reinforcer can be faded out, and the intrinsic reinforcing quality of the behavior should maintain it under the new conditions.

Selecting a Discriminative Stimulus.   For most purposes one should select an S^D (the discriminative stimulus or relevant cues) to which access can be controlled. Thus, the S^D can be used as a conditioned reinforcer to strengthen desired behaviors or weaken undesired behaviors through, for example, a DRO or DRL strategy. It is particularly important to guard against accidental or unplanned presentations of the S^D. In some cases, a behavior may already be under stimulus control, so access to the operative S^D can easily be manipulated. Consider again the example of students talking to each other: Once this talking was under the control of the "sharing-time" sign, access to the sign was used as a reinforcer.

CONCLUSION

There are several advantages to using a stimulus-control strategy:

1. *Positive orientation:* A major advantage of stimulus control is its positive orientation. The message conveyed in this approach is that the

learner is "okay" and so is the behavior, as long as it occurs under the specified stimulus conditions. For example, with stimulus control, the message is not, "Masturbation is wrong and you are bad to do it," rather, it is, "Masturbation is okay behavior, but it is better to do it in private."

2. *Control without elimination:* Many behaviors do not need to be totally eliminated from a learner's repertoire. An example might be stereotypic responding. It may be true that certain stereotypic behavior can interfere with learning, but it is an illogical leap to assume that *all* stereotypic behavior must be eliminated. In fact, most of us engage in some type of stereotypic behavior, such as foot tapping or fingering our beards or the hair on our heads. Thus, it would seem unrealistic to expect special-needs learners to be devoid of all stereotypic behavior. Instead, it is our responsibility to teach them when and where it is okay to engage in the behavior and, if possible, how to do so in a more socially appropriate way. For example, flipping almost everything in front of one's face might be reshaped into tapping a pencil when it's available or waving a fan in warm weather.

3. *Development of conditioned reinforcers:* Stimuli that become discriminative for certain behaviors, thus setting the occasion for their occurrence, become conditioned reinforcers and can be used contingently to strengthen other behavior. Thus, if a sign sets the occasion for the reinforcement of social talk in class, then the opportunity for access to the sign can be used as positive reinforcement in a program. This is a major advantage when working with a learner for whom it is difficult to identify effective reinforcers. Contingent access to an S^D such as a sign can be used as positive reinforcement for task completion, accuracy, and rate, as well as other behaviors or low rates of responding.

4. *Facilitation of generalization:* One strategy for generalizing treatment gains across settings is to use a "training stimulus" and to introduce that stimulus in subsequent settings in which one hopes generalization will occur. This strategy for stimulus control links control over a behavior problem to an explicit and clearly identified extrinsic stimulus (the S^D). Thus, an advantage of stimulus control is that, once it has been established in one setting, it may be easier to establish control in other settings. This is particularly true if the S^D is portable. In one case, for example, a hearing-disabled client who had some residual hearing ground his teeth apparently for auditory stimulation. The grinding was brought under the discriminative control of a transistor radio with earphones in the work setting. The establishment of inhibitory control at home was achieved by the systematic introduction of the S^D (i.e., the radio) in that setting as well.

5. *Limiting reinforcement:* One advantage of establishing stimulus control over an undesired behavior is the potential it provides for preventing the occurrence of unnecessary reinforcement. If, for example, a behavior occurs under a wide variety of stimulus conditions, it may be reinforced inadvertently simply because of its proximity to stimuli and events that are present but independent of the target behavior. By establishing a stimulus that is discriminative for the target behavior, the target behavior will be reinforced only by its own consequences. Given this effect, the behavior brought under such narrow stimulus control may also be reduced in overall frequency.
6. *Social validity:* In order for the stimulus control of a behavior to be unobtrusive and attract little negative attention, careful planning is necessary. We strongly recommend that the S^D be an age-appropriate item common to the natural environment. For example:
   - A radio was used for cueing no teeth grinding.
   - A pencil was used to limit "flipping," both in terms of range of motion and frequency.
   - A special pin was used to remind a learner to talk quietly while he was working.

The major caution with stimulus-control procedures is that they normally should not be applied in cases where the behavior is serious enough to warrant complete elimination (e.g., aggression and self-injurious or destructive behaviors). This should be obvious, since, for stimulus control to be established, it is necessary for the behavior to be reinforced under the specified stimulus conditions. To reinforce aggressive, self-injurious, or destructive behaviors under any set of stimulus conditions will serve to strengthen these behaviors and increase the likelihood of someone being hurt or property being destroyed.

There are special cases, however, when a stimulus-control strategy may be employed responsibly in order to reduce and eliminate a serious behavior. For example, if an analysis of the situation shows that a serious problem behavior (e.g., self-abuse) occurs in response to many stimuli, it may at first seem that a stimulus-control procedure would be difficult to use. If, however, the behavior is inhibited under very specific conditions (such as mealtimes and in the absence of task demands), the strategy can be useful. In this situation, mealtimes and low-demand times would be the S^D conditions. By scheduling these S^D conditions consecutively and then extending them, it is possible to reduce the behavior sharply. Once the behavior is under control, the demands can be gradually reintroduced. This scenario is depicted in Figure 9.1.

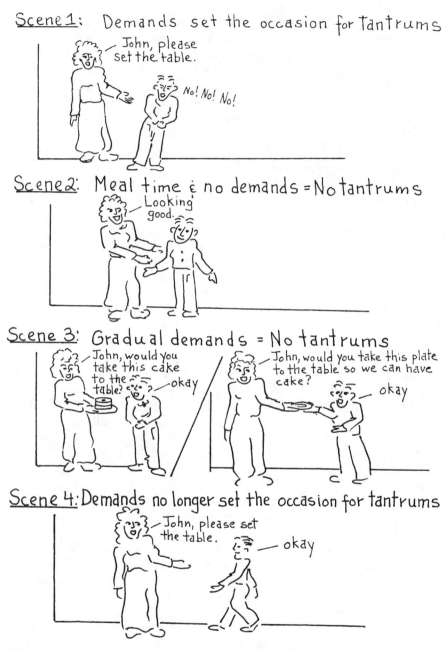

FIGURE 9.1.   Using inhibitory S^D conditions to rapidly control behavior

10

Instructional Control

Instructional control is an instance of stimulus control where a response occurs in the presence of or following the presentation of a verbal, signed, written, or otherwise explicitly communicated command, direction, request, or cue. For example, when a preschool teacher gives the direction to line up at the door and the students do so, they are under instructional control.

The strategies for establishing instructional control are similar to those for stimulus control. We have chosen to discuss instructional control at length because of its obvious importance to teachers and other "hands-on" program staff.

Instructional control is critical for staff in at least two different but not mutually exclusive ways: It is an issue in terms of behavioral deficits or "noncompliance" and in terms of specific behavior problems or "excesses." We will discuss each of these separately, although, as will be obvious, they are closely related.

USING INSTRUCTIONAL CONTROL FOR BEHAVIORAL DEFICITS OR NONCOMPLIANCE

When a learner is described as "noncompliant," it typically means that the individual did not follow a given instruction within a specified period of time and/or in the manner requested. It is important when describing a learner as noncompliant that at least the following factors be considered:

1. The behavior requested or required may not be in the person's skill repertoire. For example, a learner who is requested to put on his boots may never have been able to do this task independently.
2. The learner may have only part of the skill in her repertoire. The individual may know how to open the refrigerator but not know how to

find particular items. Thus, the instruction, "Get the milk out," may be ineffective in producing the correct response.

3. The person may have demonstrated a variety of behaviors but may never have learned the general notion of instructional control. That is, he may not understand the concept, "If I do what someone tells me, good things may happen."

4. The behavior may be in the individual's repertoire but not under instructional control. That is, she may know how to open the refrigerator and get a piece of fruit but may never have learned to connect this behavior to an instruction. When someone says, "Get the apple out of the refrigerator," then, she may appear to be "noncompliant."

5. The skill may be impossible or unreasonable to expect from the individual. No matter how great the reward or heavy the threat of punishment, most of us will not be able to win a Pulitzer Prize or climb Mt. Everest. As noted earlier, it is critical that a careful assessment be done before assuming that an individual is being noncompliant. For example, expecting a given individual to identify the time correctly as "quarter to one" may be unrealistic for him, at least at the present time. Perhaps an adaptation such as a digital clock with an alarm could be used to avoid the problem.

6. The behavior may be under instructional control but only in a given context. That is, the learner knows how to "sit at the table," but only when the instruction is given at lunch time, in the dining hall, and when the chair is moved out for her. Staff may mistakenly assume that sometimes such an individual is being noncompliant when she doesn't follow the same or a similar instruction in a totally different context.

7. The behavior may be under instructional control, but the individual may have learned it in a different manner. We have found that many individuals, and particularly those with poor social interaction and communication skills who are rigid about their routines, often learn a task in a certain way and do not understand the instruction if it is altered. For example, a person working in a stock room may know how to take the hangers out of the carton and put them on the rack but may have learned to wait for the instruction, "What do you do next?" before continuing the activity. A new staff person who does not give such a prompt may mistakenly think the individual is being noncompliant. Such situations can often be avoided by teaching tasks through the discrete-trial format (see chapters 3 and 4).

8. The individual may be capable of doing the task but simply not want to do it. No one is ever 100% compliant, nor would we want complete compliance from anyone. When this situation occurs—and it is relative-

ly rare compared to the other examples mentioned — a complete assessment of the situation is necessary. Describing such an assessment is beyond the scope of this book, but at least the following questions need to be asked:

Does she *really* need to do this task?

How many times has she had to do it today and/or in the past?

How meaningful is it to her?

Would an individual of the same age without a disability be asked to do it?

Does she have sufficient opportunity to make choices and decisions about what she does in other situations?

Discrete-Trial Format

When the behavior is not in the individual's repertoire, is only partially in the repertoire, or is only understood in one form, and/or when the person seems to have no notion of following instructions, we have found the discrete-trial format (DTF) very useful (see chapter 3). The critical aspects of this teaching format are summarized as follows:

1. Obtain the learner's attention
2. Present the instructional stimulus
3. Immediately prompt a correct response before allowing an incorrect one to occur
4. Deliver positive reinforcement following the occurrence of the correct response
5. Wait a sufficient length of time before presenting the next instructional stimulus, so the learner can discriminate each trial as a discrete event unconnected to the trials that precede and follow it
6. Fade the prompt gradually, over subsequent trials

Here are some examples of situations using the DTF:

- A child who never put on his boots was first instructed to do so and then prompted through the parts of the task with which he was having difficulty.
- A learner was taught to find specific items in the refrigerator. At first the prompt was a "within stimulus prompt" with the milk the only item on the shelf. Gradually, more items were added and more could be requested.

For individuals who do not understand how to follow instructions, using a teaching format such as the DTF, which clearly spells out the relationship between instruction and payoff, can begin to teach instruction-following behaviors.

Further, when a learner knows a task in one form only, staff can do a complete stimulus change (see chapter 11) and reteach a sequence using DTF. The stock room staff assigned one learner to a different part of the site with a different task and taught him without verbal and inadvertent prompts, through the DTF.

Differential Reinforcement

In addition to the DTF, staff can use differential reinforcement strategies to establish instructional control over a particular behavior and begin to help the learner make the connection between following directions and good things happening. Using differential reinforcement strategies, staff reinforce the behavior when it occurs following an instruction (verbal or otherwise) and ignore the behavior when it occurs without an instructional cue. This strategy is useful particularly when the behavior already occurs at a reasonable rate and does not need prompting. The following examples will help illustrate this point:

- A differential reinforcement strategy was used with Mary. She would go to the refrigerator fairly often but did not do so under instruction. Staff began asking her to go to the refrigerator often. When she complied, she was reinforced; but when she did not comply or when she went to the refrigerator spontaneously, she was ignored. Of course, if assessment had shown that she seldom went to the refrigerator on her own, staff would have had to prompt the behavior through the discrete-trial format.
- Bill seemed to have no notion of instructional control but exhibited some behaviors at very high rates. Bill's mother "inserted" an instruction often for certain of these behaviors and reinforced the first response following the instruction. For instance, Bill was constantly closing open cabinets and doors. His mother left some doors ajar and, as Bill went to close them, said, "Bill, close the door on the cupboard, please." Similarly, she said, "Bill, close the front door, please," several times a day. Even though Bill was likely to have closed the doors anyway, his mother reinforced the behavior when it followed an instruction. The same procedure was then used to reinforce other behaviors already occurring at fairly high rates, to help Bill develop the notion of instructional control.

USING INSTRUCTIONAL CONTROL FOR EXCESS BEHAVIOR

Instructional control procedures can also be used in those instances in which the behavior is in the repertoire but is inappropriate.

Discrete-Trial Format

Using the DTF to establish instructional control is effective in dealing with excess behaviors in at least three ways:

To teach behaviors that are incompatible with the problem behavior
To do what is referred to as "compliance training"
To develop generalized instructional control

The following are examples of cases where the DTF can be used to gain instructional control over excess behavior:

- A vocational training instructor was interested in teaching a student to comply with a basic command to "sit down" in order to reduce out-of-seat behavior, which was disruptive to the job site and rendered the student inaccessible to the instructional/training process.
- Mike engaged in several excess behaviors. In "compliance training," Mike was taught the appropriate response to various instructions such as, "Put the dishes on the table" and "Open the boxes now," and was reinforced for correct responding. This had the effect of indirectly reducing his excess behaviors as it has been found that increasing the ability of the individual to respond correctly to a variety of instructions often can reduce indirect inappropriate behaviors.

Other students who exhibited tantrums, biting, hair pulling, and the like also were taught systematically to comply to reasonable commands. Likewise, as a result, these behavior problems diminished.

In generalized instructional control, the systematic teaching of correct responses to instructions becomes so successful that each new response takes less time to learn. The instructional control has generalized when the learner responds to a novel instruction the first time. Thus, if a person responds correctly to the instruction, "hands down," the first time he hears it, generalized instructional control or generalized compliance is said to have been established. Naturally, this generalized compliance can be useful, particularly for teaching clients in community settings. Here, novel events that may cause a learner embarrassment or put him in danger can occur, and instructions can be given to avoid such consequences. On the other hand, although generalized instructional control is important, one would not want to have so much control that learners become automatons.

Differential Reinforcement Strategies

The use of differential reinforcement has been discussed already as it relates to teaching compliance. It also may be used to reduce and control excess behavior, and the issues are essentially the same. It is best used as a strategy for dealing with annoying but not dangerous behaviors. A good example is Bill's cupboard-door-closing behavior, which might be a high-rate, disruptive, but certainly not dangerous, behavior. Once such behavior is brought under instructional control through differential reinforcement, the instruction can be faded out so the learner receives only an occasional opportunity to follow that instruction and be reinforced. The following is a case in point:

- Sam lived with several other young men. He was in the habit of moving small pieces of furniture around as often as 20 times in an evening. His housemates began to tell him, "Sam, move that end-table over here," "Move that chair," and so forth, each time he began to move a piece of furniture. He would, naturally, comply, and they would differentially thank him. After some time they began to decrease the number of times they asked him to move things and finally were asking him only to move things that really needed to be moved, such as the chairs at dinner, trash cans, tables to make room for a game, and the like.

SUGGESTIONS FOR IMPLEMENTING INSTRUCTIONAL CONTROL

The following suggestions for implementation emanate from our own experience and that of others. These include:

1. Basic learner assessment
2. Demand-giving style and instructional input
3. Generalization
4. Selecting behaviors
5. Natural settings

Each of these will be discussed briefly.

Basic Learner Assessment.   There are basic types of information which are necessary to have before trying to establish or increase instructional control. Among these are the learner's visual and auditory ability, the learner's modality preference, and the learner's language comprehension. You also may observe that some learners need additional time to process instructional requests. Giving them extra time usually means they will comply when they can. Time allotted should be reasonable and based on an individual's needs.

The first step in the basic assessment is to determine the learner's understanding of directions. It has been our experience, even with the most disruptive learners, that problems may not be due to noncompliance but rather to the inability to understand and make sense of the instructions being given. Determine which directions the learner currently will follow and the extent to which she will do so. This is valuable information for designing a systematic approach that will increase instructional control and cultivate generalized compliance.

Direction-Giving Style and Instructional Input. Direction-giving style can contribute to behavior problems. In some cases, a person delivering the instruction may not have a style that naturally conveys confidence and a firm expectation of compliance. This lack often results in noncompliance. In most instructional situations, the goal is to convey the message, "Do what I tell you and there will be a payoff." To get this message across as effectively as possible, keep the following points in mind:

Be clear
Be brief
Be firm, but nice

Many instructors have reported experience in which learners will perform for one person but not another. Often this is because one person is unsure of himself and not confident that the learner can/will perform the task requested. If someone does not have good instructional style, coaching him may be helpful. If it isn't, it may be necessary to find someone else to conduct the training program.

Remember, the more the learner is challenged by cognitive and/or language difficulties, the more you have to make sure the instruction you are giving makes sense to *that* learner. Table 10.1 gives examples of good and bad instructions.

Sometimes learners make sense of their world more easily if the instruction is given visually. Laying out the task in the natural sequence, giving a series of pictures of what comes next, and using exaggerated modeling have all been found useful for individuals who do not seem to understand just through "telling." (See "Adaptations" section in the bibliography.)

TABLE 10.1. Examples of good and bad instructions for learners with cognitive and language difficulties

Good Instructions	Bad Instructions
Bob, put your toys in the box and come sit at the table.	Now Bob, get your things together very neatly, nicely, and quietly, and then show me you're ready for snack time. That's better.
Fold the towel, Helen. Match this corner to that one.	Now try folding this here for me. Just bend it in half and make it smaller.
Match it, please.	Find the one that looks just like the one in the picture, and then you'll know where to put the one you have.

Sometimes a learner may be under limited instructional control but still appear to be noncompliant or may exhibit problem behaviors. When this occurs, the problem may be with the format of the instruction, that is, with how the instructions are being given. Variables to consider include

1. Content (what is being said)
2. Medium (written, verbal, signed, etc.)
3. Brevity
4. Clarity
5. Conciseness
6. Timing of presentation

We have found that some individuals with severe learning or language difficulties may be under the control of the written word more than the spoken word. Therefore, if we cannot achieve compliance with our spoken requests, instructions, demands, and rules, it is helpful sometimes to see where presentation in a written or other format will make the difference.

Generalization. It is important that instructional control be generalized across a wide range of relevant dimensions. In order to know that instructional control has been established firmly, it has to be demonstrated in the following ways:

1. *Across a number of settings:* The instruction "put it on . . . " could be used in a grocery store when loading groceries, in a laundry room when

loading laundry, in the kitchen when cooking, in the playroom when cleaning up, and so forth.

2. *Across a number of persons:* A learner should be able to follow a directive given by his teacher, parent, or other appropriate community person.

3. *At different times of day:* A person should be able to respond to the directive to "get dressed" in the morning before work, in the afternoon after swimming, and so forth.

4. *For different forms of the instructional stimulus:* To the extent possible, the instructional stimulus should be varied to the degree that variation occurs in the natural environment. For example, a person should be able to respond to varied requests for orders given by different restaurant personnel, such as, "Can I help you?" "Order please" and "What would you like?"

5. *For different content:* Generalization on this dimension would include comprehension of instructions such as, "Put the food in the cart," "Put the clothes in the basket," and "Put the toys away."

6. *For varying immediacy of reinforcement delivery:* Learners should respond to immediate and delayed reinforcement, as in "As soon as you put your toys away you may have a snack," or "Put your toys away and later you can make a snack."

7. *For different proximities between the learner and the teacher:* This variable is critical, especially when independence is the ultimate goal. For example, a learner should be able to perform her vocational task, whether the instructor or supervisor is present or not.

Selecting Behaviors.   In selecting behaviors to bring under instructional control, the behavior to be reinforced should be one that is incompatible with whatever problem behaviors the learner is exhibiting and it should be enforceable. It also should be one that can be prompted or one that exists already and can be easily reinforced.

Natural Settings.   As discussed, a model that we have found effective for establishing compliance in a variety of natural settings is discrete-trial training. To use this in natural settings, you first develop a list of requests or directions the learner is to follow. The requests should be age-appropriate and functional. Ask yourself, what kinds of requests would normally be made of a person of this age in this environment? Then present the learner with each of these requests or directions at least once a day, using the discrete-trial format. The learner's attention should be obtained and the instructional stimulus should be presented clearly and distinctly. The wording of the requests should remain reasonably similar. Staff should wait for compliance without repeating the request. For example:

- Staff were interested in being able to take Monica to fast-food restaurants. They generated the following list of instructions:

  Get in line
  Wait
  Tell me what you're going to have
  Let's sit here
  Let's go
  Open the door, please.

  She worked on these every opportunity she had, across as many environments and activities as possible, and others (family included) did the same.

Remember to keep the following points in mind:

Determine the instructions ahead of time
Keep instructions the same across people
Repeat the sequence across the day when possible

If the learner complies within the specified time frame, a significant positive reinforcer should be delivered. If the learner does not comply, the staff member should continue on with the day's routine without comment. Many times this simple process of differential reinforcement is effective in establishing instructional control. If this approach is not effective, a prompt/prompt-fading component can be added.

CONCLUSION

There are a number of advantages to instructional control as a strategy for reducing problem behaviors in applied settings, including the following:

1. *Positive and constructive orientation:* Instructional control is a positive strategy and does not require the use of an aversive stimulus or of contingent withdrawal of a reinforcing stimulus. In addition, instructional control also is constructive. It teaches the learner a set of responses alternative to and competitive with the undesirable behavior. Further, to the extent that a learner is under instructional control, that control can be used to teach a wide range of behaviors.
2. *Efficiency:* Instructional control is a highly efficient intervention strategy. For example, it is possible that other inappropriate behaviors may

decrease as instructional control increases. In addition, developing instructional control may require decreasing amounts of time for the learner to reach a criterion level of performance for each subsequent and new request included in the training program.

3. *Social validity:* There are a number of reasons why instructional control would be widely accepted by the community at large. Most significantly, instructional control is a "natural" intervention strategy. That is, it employs signs, rules, instructions, and the like, all of which our society, in general, uses most prominently to control all of our behavior. Some common examples are shown in Figure 10.1.

4. *Rapidity of effectiveness:* Instructional control can contribute to the rapid management of problem behavior, as in the following case:
   - An adolescent with autism had problems keeping his hands to himself when walking through the halls between classes. Since he *always* followed any rule that was written down, his school counselor simply added the rule, "No touching in hallways," to his high school handbook and the problem was solved.

FIGURE 10.1.   Examples of written and spoken instructions common in the natural environment

There are three major cautions regarding the use of instructional control as a strategy for management of human behavior:

1. *Forced responding:* The first caution involves the use of prompting and prompt fading as a strategy for establishing instructional control. Danger exists if the prompt is physical and involves "motoring" the learner through the responses. If the learner actively resists the prompt and if it escalates to the point of the learner physically being forced to respond, we will have crossed the line and begun to use "forced responding," an aversive intervention. As a nonaversive strategy, we recommend the development of instructional control using differential reinforcement and prompting *without* forced responding.

2. *Generalization:* The second caution concerns the fact that practitioners occasionally equate instructional control over a behavior with the terminal or ultimate goal. The danger is that this too-limited notion of instructional control potentially restricts the learner to those situations in which particular staff members or instructional stimuli are located. While this may be necessary at first, it is important to consider the learner's current and subsequent environments and, to the maximum extent possible, fade to more natural cues. For example:

   • A teacher's aide was working with a student who was learning to vacuum. They practiced in the teacher's lounge, and the teacher's aide pointed out spots the student had missed. The teacher's aide did not consider that a subsequent environment would be an un-

FIGURE 10.2.   Until the learner can be successful in the absence of the instructional stimuli, training is incomplete

supervised apartment. This student needed to be able to vacuum without someone there to help him. The aide was helped to plan systematically for teaching independence in this task. The failure to consider this point can result in a scene such as that shown in Figure 10.2.

3. *Generalized instructional control versus automaton behavior:* As noted earlier in this chapter, we are always concerned that generalized instructional control will be misinterpreted as a need to control completely the behavior of the learner. It is important that all learners be allowed to make choices and have appropriate autonomy over their lifestyles.

11

Stimulus Change and Stimulus Satiation

STIMULUS CHANGE

Stimulus change is the sudden and noncontingent introduction of a new stimulus or a dramatic alteration of the stimulus conditions, resulting in a temporary period of target response reduction. It is important to stress that the introduction of the new stimulus is not contingent upon or related to the occurrence of the target behavior. For example:

- A student's high rate of talk-outs and other problematic verbal behavior was dramatically affected by the appearance of a substitute teacher. After 1 week, however, the behavior returned to its original rate.

Stimulus-change effects are usually dramatic but temporary. Most staff members have noted that when some learners enter a new program or classroom they seem to "behave" for a short period of time before their problem behaviors reported from a previous setting reappear. This is known colloquially as the "honeymoon effect." Though often noted, however, this honeymoon effect is seldom considered as a procedure that can help solve a problem behavior. In this section we will discuss it as a stimulus-change procedure.

A stimulus-change procedure typically results in a general reduction of many responses in the learner's repertoire, including the undesired one. This reduction in the undesired response is only temporary. If the original contingencies are maintained, the behavior will reappear. If the period of temporary response reduction is used to establish a new contingency, the behavior often can be prevented from returning to its previous strength. Stimulus change is most effective in controlling undesired behaviors when paired with new contingencies. Here is an illustration:

- The vocational teacher in a new program decided to take advantage of the change in behavior which he knew would occur during the honeymoon period. He used the temporary reduction of fighting in the vocational site to establish a token economy to reinforce the absence of fighting and the use of appropriate social interaction skills.

In some situations stimulus change is used to establish a lull in which to provide an opportunity to implement a new procedure in what may seem to be an unending stream of undesired behaviors. Teachers have used a stimulus-change procedure successfully to interrupt very-high-rate behavior. For example:

- An adolescent with autism asked incessant repetitive and nonsensical questions. It was difficult to establish a behavioral procedure because the rate of question asking was so high. Nothing worked until one morning when the teacher produced a dramatic change by moving both his desk and the student's desk to the school parking lot. The student's question asking (and all other verbal behavior) came to a standstill long enough for a successful procedure to be introduced.

Suggestions for Implementing Stimulus Change

Though underutilized, stimulus change is a very useful procedure. If understood, it can be used to advantage when it naturally occurs and can also be engineered when needed to deal with a crisis or the unexpected.

Naturally Occurring Opportunities.   It is wise to take advantage of naturally occurring opportunities where one can anticipate the honeymoon effect. If a learner is moved to a new setting and the undesired behavior is not occurring, you should start an intervention program before the behavior reappears. This strategy was used in the following example:

- Staff at a group home were warned that they could expect Brunhilda, a new arrival and a truly notorious learner, to be a handful. When Brunhilda appeared, however, all seemed well for the first 2 days. Instead of waiting for trouble to begin, the staff decided to introduce an Alt-R procedure based on information available from the student's records. They particularly concentrated reinforcement strategies on any successful completion of chores and appropriate social behavior, as the alternative negative behaviors had been major problems for her in other homes. They combined this with a DRO procedure in which she was offered a variety of preferred after-dinner activities because she'd had such a good day. Her problem behaviors almost never occurred in her new home.

Dramatic Stimulus.   When using a planned stimulus-change strategy, the new or altered stimulus should be as dramatic as possible. Some examples might include

> Wearing a new, somewhat outlandish outfit to work one day
> Totally rearranging the room — chairs, tables, beds, desks — in one day
> Trying new community environments
> Bringing breakfast to class one morning

Delaying Tactic.   If serious behavior problems are occurring, a stimulus-change procedure may allow the time needed for a more complete assessment of the behavior and development and implementation of an intervention plan. In addition, such an approach may provide at least some temporary relief for staff. For example:
- Holly was moved to a new classroom after experiencing limited success in reducing tantrum behavior. In the new location, Holly's inappropriate behavior decreased significantly, long enough for a successful DRO procedure to be implemented.

Initial Boost.   By combining stimulus change with other treatment strategies, you can start an intervention strategy positively. This provides an increased opportunity for the learner to receive reinforcement contingent upon the display of desired behavior. Immediate reinforcement for the staff through rapid initial success for implementing and carrying through with an intervention strategy also is provided. The previous example involving Brunhilda is a good example. The honeymoon effect was used to boost the effects of an Alt-R procedure for reinforcing any successful completion of tasks and appropriate social behaviors.

Crisis Intervention.   The dramatic introduction of a new stimulus may startle a learner and produce enough disruption to aggressive, self-injurious, or property-destruction behavior that it precludes the necessity for physical intervention and minimizes the possibility for injury.

Respite Work.   Respite workers who provide services to families of persons who display problem behaviors usually do not have time to develop long-term interventions. Where there is no usable, ongoing intervention strategy, respite workers can use stimulus change. The respite workers themselves may even act as a stimulus change.

Substitute Teaching.   A substitute teacher typically has difficulty controlling student behavior; in fact, his mere presence may trigger inappropriate behaviors. He could use a stimulus-change procedure to get the students' attention long enough to explain the plans and contingency rules that will be in effect during his tenure. Some ideas for stimulus change include bringing the class a special food treat, tapes of popular music to play, or some special games.

Planned Novelty.   Changing wall decorations and rearranging furniture at home or work can produce a period of relatively good behavior in learners and provide an opportunity to implement any new long-term strategies that may be necessary for serious problem behaviors.

Added Opportunity.   The effects of stimulus change can create additional opportunities for utilization of other nonaversive strategies. For example, if a behavior is occurring at such high rates that a DRO procedure is not practical, a stimulus change could make such an approach possible. The stimulus change can immediately disrupt the target behavior and provide experiences for immediate reinforcement on a new schedule, as was the case in the following example:

- A young man, Mike, hit himself when he was not permitted access to a certain board game. Whenever he began hitting himself, a person who lived with him turned on loud music. When the music started, Mike stopped hitting, and the person with whom he lived showed him a picture schedule to help Mike know when he could play the game.

Nonrecurring Problems.   Most intervention strategies are developed to deal with behavior over time. They are not applicable in situations where behaviors occur as isolated, unexpected, nonrecurring problems. Stimulus change can be useful in a situation where a learner is having a tantrum and does not typically display this behavior. In this situation one could flick the lights on or off or begin to sing, in order to elicit a stimulus-change effect when a problem occurs.

Advantages and Cautions

There are two major advantages to using a stimulus-change procedure.

1. *Speed of effects:* If stimulus change works at all in reducing a behavior problem, it works immediately. If a stimulus change does not disrupt the behavior immediately, it is unlikely to do so at all. It is possible, of

course, to try a new and different stimulus. For example, vocational instructors just beginning community training with special education learners often find that, despite their worst fears, the change to non-school environments actually reduces problem behaviors. If this change is not sufficient, they can try other changes, such as using the city bus, trying a different grocery store, and so forth.

2. *Crisis strategy:* The immediacy of its effect gives stimulus change its second advantage, its usefulness in crisis situations, such as when a behavior presents a serious threat to health, safety, or property. In such situations a stimulus change may

>Provide a temporary reduction in the problem behaviors, allowing time for a behavioral assessment
>Provide time for the development of an intervention plan
>Prevent injury or damage until a more permanent solution can be found
>Provide additional opportunity for alternative strategies
>Facilitate rapid, permanent control over a behavior problem if used in combination with another intervention strategy

An example of the use of stimulus change as a crisis strategy is as follows:

- One residential program succeeded in interrupting high-rate disruptive behavior of adolescents by boarding up the recreation room for three days. Signs were posted in dramatic fashion: "Wait 'til Friday!" These very disturbed students had a dramatically lower rate of problem behaviors for three days. They spent most of the 3 days talking and wondering about the room, rather than engaging in aggressive and troublesome behavior. After that time, the staff introduced a new recreation room with many games. Access to games and other recreation equipment could be obtained through earning points in the new token economy system.

Cautions regarding the use of stimulus change include the following:

1. *Temporary effects:* A dramatic change or presentation of a new stimulus can cause a disruption in the display of the undesired behavior. If the old contingencies maintaining the behavior still are present, however, the behaviors will reappear. If a permanent reduction in problem behaviors is desired, contingencies must be changed by the introduction of a well-thought-out management program based on a thorough functional analysis of the conditions surrounding the behavior. Stimulus change as an intervention strategy is quite limited as to what it can

accomplish, and in most instances it must be used in combination with another intervention strategy.

2. *Adaptation:* The effective presentation of stimulus change may be limited for those who readily adapt to change and for whom the noncontingent introduction of a new stimulus does not have a disruptive effect on behavior. Also, if stimulus change is used repeatedly, an individual may "learn" that such changes are not related to behavior and thus come to disregard them. For example:

   - Jamie displayed a "honeymoon effect" when entering a new classroom but started misbehaving after one week. The "honeymoon effect" was limited and did not repeat itself indefinitely, even when classroom changes were scheduled on a weekly basis.

STIMULUS SATIATION

Stimulus satiation involves the continuous and noncontingent availability of the reinforcer that is identified as maintaining the undesired behavior, thereby weakening its effectiveness and reducing the rate of the defined behavior.

It is important to distinguish between stimulus satiation and negative practice overcorrection. The latter, which we do not recommend, requires that each time the learner engages in the problem or negative behavior, she continue performing it over and over again. This differs from stimulus satiation in that negative practice overcorrection

1. Requires forced responding and repetition of the undesired behavior each time it occurs
2. Is contingent upon the occurrence of undesired behavior
3. Does not specifically identify the reinforcer or change the level of access to it
4. Is considered an aversive procedure, due to the element of forced responding

The following two examples contrast the two procedures, to further clarify these distinctions.

   - *Negative practice overcorrection:* Steven's teacher reported that he was ripping paper in the classroom at a high rate. These were his own, his classmates', and the teacher's papers. Each time Steven demonstrated the behavior of ripping paper, he was required to rip more paper repeatedly, for an extended period of time. (We would

prefer to use a DRL or DRO procedure rather than negative practice overcorrection to deal with this problem in a positive way.)
- *Stimulus satiation:* An elementary teacher had a problem with her
  6- and 7-year-old students, who were continually out of their seats
  and going over to the side of the room to peek at the rabbits and
  hamsters she brought in for them. The animals were kept covered
  because she thought they would be less distracting to the children,
  but, instead, the covers seemed to increase the students' interest and
  consequent out-of-seat behavior. Using a stimulus-satiation procedure, this teacher removed the covers from the animal cages. After
  the first few days of continuous access to the animals, the students
  stopped going over to the cages, except during playtime.

Suggestions for Implementing Stimulus Satiation

In order for stimulus satiation to be used effectively as an intervention
for reducing behavior, certain conditions must be met.

1. The reinforcer maintaining the desired behavior must be clearly
   defined.
2. The reinforcement must be noncontingently available.
3. The reinforcer must be made available either continuously or at
   least more often than would be chosen, given free access.

These conditions suggest that a stimulus-satiation procedure would be
best implemented when the reinforcer

1. Can be made available indefinitely
2. Can be made available at high levels
3. Is part of the person's natural environment
4. Is used in combination with positive programming

Stimulus satiation was used effectively in this example:
- A targeted goal for Jack was to decrease the number of times he
  went for a drink of water. There was no medical reason for his
  behavior. Initially, this occurred at a very high frequency and was
  interfering with Jack's ability to participate in daily school routines
  and instruction. Once it was determined that opportunities for a
  drink were, in fact, maintaining that behavior, Jack was given
  unlimited and noncontingent opportunity to drink by keeping a
  pitcher of water filled by his desk. When given this continuous
  access, satiation occurred and Jack stopped going to get a drink.

Limitations

In comparison with other strategies for reducing behavior problems, stimulus satiation has more limited application, for the following reasons:

1. Use of this intervention strategy requires that time be spent carrying out a thorough functional analysis, of course, but it is often difficult to identify accurately the reinforcer maintaining the undesired behavior, as in the following example:
   - An initial observation led staff to believe that Lee's hoarding of buttons was being maintained by actual collection of the buttons. A further and more detailed analysis indicated that the attention Lee received for hoarding was what actually maintained the behavior. While we think functional analysis is always important, it may be difficult to identify correctly the reinforcer to use in a satiation procedure.
2. Often, successful results of this strategy have only a temporary effect on reducing the undesired behavior, unless the reinforcer can be provided continually at very high levels.
3. Given a particular environment or circumstance, it is often not possible or natural to provide the reinforcer at high enough levels over an extended period of time, in order to produce the effect of satiation (Figure 11.1).

There probably aren't enough shoes in the world to satiate little Imelda.

FIGURE 11.1.   Stimulus satiation may require levels of reinforcement that are impractical or even impossible

12

Additive Procedures

Additive procedures involve the combining of two or more procedures in order to reduce or eliminate an undesired behavior. Consider this example:

- Mark demonstrated severe aggression and destructive behavior. The first program used an Alt-R procedure in which the student was reinforced for behaviors that were incompatible with aggression and destruction. With this approach the behavior came under considerable control; however, there were still some episodes of aggression, as shown in Figure 12.1. Rather than scrapping this procedure and beginning a new one, the support person decided to *add* a procedure to help Mark gain additional control. In this case the goal was to help him control his outbursts for extended periods of time. The support worker decided the best way to accomplish this was with a DRO progressive procedure. Thus, in addition to the reinforcement Mark received for performing specified alternative behaviors, he was reinforced for going consecutive periods of time with no aggressive or destructive incidents. As Figure 12.2 shows, this eventually led to the elimination of the target behaviors.

VARIATIONS OF ADDITIVE PROCEDURES

The variations of additive procedures are virtually unlimited. Each of the various procedures discussed in this book can be effectively combined with others to create an even more effective program, if the situation calls for it. As emphasized throughout this book, all procedures, whether used singly or in combination, should be used in conjunction with positive programming. Also, as discussed in chapter 2 and elsewhere in this book, always remember to assess the possible communicative functions of any undesirable behavior. It may be the learner's only way of telling us he's confused, bored, angry, and so forth. For more information on determin-

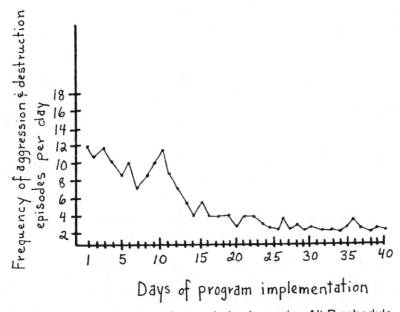

FIGURE 12.1.   Reduction of target behaviors using Alt-R schedule alone

ing possible message value of such behaviors, see Donnellan, Mirenda, Mesaros, and Fassbender (1984) in the "Positive Programming" section of the bibliography. Attempts to eliminate behaviors without providing students with a different means to communicate their message will likely result in new (and perhaps more severe) behavior problems. The following example summarizes a case where an additive procedure was used combining stimulus change with a DRO schedule:

- Tom made noises to himself while working. He had done so for quite some time in many different environments, but at this particular job site it was very disruptive to other workers and was stigmatizing for Tom. He had been instructed to stop and a DRO procedure had been attempted. The frequency of the noises was so high, however, that the DRO was difficult to implement.

  The job trainer decided that what was needed was a temporary reduction of the behavior so the staff could use the DRO procedure. Stimulus change was chosen as the best way of producing this effect. On the first morning of the new program, Tom came to his work station as usual. His job trainer told him that, instead of beginning his work right away, he

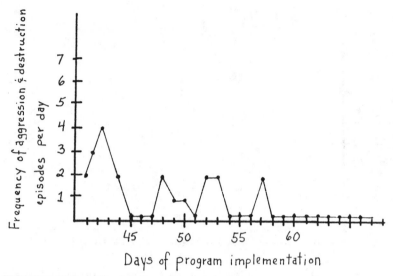

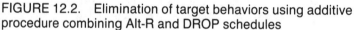

Days of program implementation

FIGURE 12.2.   Elimination of target behaviors using additive
procedure combining Alt-R and DROP schedules

was to do a couple of errands for his supervisor first. This change served
to reduce the noise making long enough for the job trainer to implement
the DRO program. For each day of the first week of the program, the
trainer devised some way of having Tom start the day just a little differently than the day before. By the end of the week the DRO program was
beginning to control the noise making, so the stimulus-change aspect
was dropped.

Additional examples of the effective use of additive procedures follow:

• Jimmy was shy and rarely interacted with other children. There were a
few times during the day when he hovered around other children and
appeared to be at least somewhat interested in what they were doing.
His recess supervisor wanted to use an Alt-R procedure to increase such
interactions, but so few occurred that he felt it would not result quickly
enough in the kind of change he wanted to see. He decided to combine
the Alt-R schedule with a shaping procedure. Through shaping, he began to change Jimmy's hovering into participation. As Jimmy moved
closer to the group, the recess supervisor reinforced things such as touching the materials, touching other children, asking questions, and making comments (see Figure 12.3). Through the Alt-R procedure, these
behaviors were reinforced so that their frequency increased.

- John was a sloppy student. He did not work neatly, groom himself, or keep his belongings together. This resulted in his losing many of his things as well as in an inappropriate appearance, especially when out in the community. It was a problem both his family and his teacher were interested in changing. John wanted very much to be able to begin wearing a watch, which, of course, his family was afraid he would lose. John's teacher decided to use a combination of (1) positive programming, (2) instructional control, (3) stimulus control, and (4) Alt-R.

  As part of positive programming, they worked on various areas of hygiene, including John washing two loads of his clothing a week and posting a cleanliness checklist on the refrigerator that John checked before leaving in the morning.

  As part of instructional control, his teacher and family instructed John to put his clothes in his closet, to clean the dishes after he cooked, to comb his hair and tuck in his shirt before leaving the classroom, and the like.

  He received reinforcement for following through with all of these behaviors when he was wearing his watch (stimulus control). He could

FIGURE 12.3. Examples of behaviors for which Jimmy was reinforced through a combination of shaping and Alt-R

choose to be messy at certain times during the day (e.g., recess) and during certain activities (e.g., a messy craft activity), but during those times he was not to wear the watch. Over time he learned that when he was wearing his watch he needed to look clean and neat, to work neatly, and to take care of materials.

SUGGESTIONS FOR IMPLEMENTING ADDITIVE PROCEDURES

As mentioned previously, it is essential that all procedures be used in combination with positive programming. Behaviors do not occur in a vacuum, nor can we attempt to modify them as if they do. It is our task to provide learners with a stimulating, meaningful, and chronological-age-appropriate curriculum, within which we can then help them learn to control problem behaviors. Any combining of strategies will be effective only if we are concurrently helping students learn new behaviors and skills.

The most obvious time to use additive procedures is when a single intervention strategy, in addition to positive programming, has had measurable but insufficient effect on a problem. You also may decide from the very beginning that more than one procedure will be the most effective strategy.

CONCLUSION

The advantage of using additive procedures is that the effectiveness of the treatment program can be greatly increased. Results may be quicker, stronger, and/or longer lasting.

The only caution regarding additive procedures is that it is then difficult to evaluate the effectiveness of the application of any one approach. This is most important for experimental work, but may be important in applied work as well, since staff need to be able to relay information regarding the most effective strategy with a particular student. When using additive procedures, only the entire treatment package can be evaluated.

Conclusion

The material we have presented is intended as a guide for teachers, staff, parents, and others having ongoing responsibility for learners who present challenging behaviors, though we believe the book will also be useful to teacher trainers and other staff development professionals. The examples we used were drawn from our own experiences and those of our friends and colleagues; details were, of course, changed to protect the privacy of the individuals involved. As we noted in the Introduction, this book is not meant to be a conceptual work on the subject; references to our conceptual work and other information on the topic can be found in the Bibliography, which also contains further sources on each of the procedures we have discussed. We would like to emphasize that in the preceding chapters we have not attempted solutions to all the individual problems that may be encountered, some of which will surely require direct intervention or supervision by experienced professionals skilled in nonaversive behavioral strategies. Readers are encouraged to contact us if they are unable to find professional assistance that utilizes nonaversive techniques to deal with severe behavior problems. We will endeavor to provide information about literature, professionals, and state-of-the-art resources in the field.

In this book we have presented both teaching techniques and management strategies. All these individual procedures are reasonable alternatives to the use of punishment. Used in combination and in the context of positive programming, their effectiveness can often be greatly increased. Positive programming entails both an adequate assessment and the teaching of replacement behaviors and functionally equivalent behaviors.

For us *positive* also means that any intervention for changing or managing challenging behavior must take place in the context of a program that promotes meaningful, age-appropriate, functional skill development in natural settings. Sources of information on the development of such programs are presented in the Bibliography. We sincerely believe that positive programs—based on proper assessment and backed up by professional expertise that is available as necessary — can always make it unnecessary to resort to using aversive interventions. Certainly that has been our experience and the experience of the hundreds of parents and professionals with whom we have worked over the past several years.

In reflecting back on the experience of those years, we have come to realize that there is one more essential ingredient that has helped to make our work successful, exciting, and fascinating for us: We have always endeavored to understand the situation from the perspective of the individual who is exhibiting the behavior problem. Often this is a difficult task because many of our learners have an inadequate or at least idiosyncratic understanding of the world due to their unusual life and treatment histories, as well as to their learning problems. And typically they have communication and other handicapping conditions that make it difficult or even impossible to ask them directly about situations. As can be seen from many of the questions we presented under "Assessment" in Chapter 1, the effort to glean such information requires that we go beyond the obvious and immediately available data. Always, of course, we utilize an empirical approach and attempt to support our hypotheses about the individual's perspective through systematic changes and careful attention to the data generated. Nonetheless, it must be said that in many situations in which we have dealt successfully with complex behavior problems, we have been willing to consider alternative explanations even if these do not immediately present themselves within our behavioral framework and our understanding of the successful interventions presented in the literature.

Consider, for example, how different the experience of placement in a group home might be for a learner who comes from an institutional back ward and one who has had an interesting, varied life in a good family situation. For the former, the activities and expectations of a good group home may be overwhelming; for the latter, they may be boring. On the other hand, the learner from the institution may have lost everyone he knew throughout his lifetime when he moved to the home, whereas the family of the learner who came from her own home may continue to visit on a weekly basis. Even if both of these learners were to exhibit the same serious behavior problem, their situations would probably have to be addressed differently because they are different people with very different experiences. These personal life experiences may or may not be the critical variables in solving a particular behavior problem, but they need to be addressed, as do many other questions related to the personal perspective of the individual learner who is presenting a behavioral challenge.

This approach is well illustrated in a story told by Tom Willis of the Institute for Applied Behavior Analysis about a woman who has been operating a foster home for exceptional learners for many years. Not long ago she took an 8-year-old girl in her care and discovered that the child would not eat anything except pizza and chocolate ice cream. The woman was, of course, concerned about the limited nutritional value of such a diet, so she contacted the agency that had referred the child to her. A psychologist specializing in behavior problems came to her home and determined that the child was being noncompliant; the psychologist developed a program in which the child would be given her meal and then required to sit at the table until she ate it. If a reasonable length of time passed and the girl had not eaten her food, it would be removed; however, the same food would be presented to the child at the next meal. This would continue until she ate the food or it spoiled, at which point the process would start again with the new food.

By mid-week the little girl had consistently refused all the food presented to her and was losing a substantial amount of weight. The foster mother was starting to panic. Then she remembered that the child had a rather checkered history: She had been raised by a single mother who was desperately trying to scratch out a living and care for this child, who had a significant disability. The foster mother surmised that the child had probably been given pizza and ice cream as her main meal so often that she had come to believe that real food must look like pizza and ice cream. To test her notion she decided to continue to feed the child pizza, but to put on the pizza other things she wanted the girl to eat, such as green vegetables. Sure enough, the little girl ate the vegetables; in fact, she would eat anything, as long as it was served on pizza. She was served more and more things on the pizza, and the pizza itself was gradually faded out. The final result was that the child would eat a wide range of foods even if the pizza was not present. The foster mother employed a similar strategy with the ice cream, gradually thinning it with milk until the child was eventually able to drink anything.

Certainly, we can explain the success of this foster mother in terms of fading procedures and other techniques presented in this book. Here, however, we want to emphasize instead that the technology worked because the woman was able to go beyond the reported studies on "noncompliance" and "eating disorders" and to reframe the questions into: "What would cause a child to do this?" "What was her life like up to this point?" "What might she think is going on here?"

From stories such as this we have learned to ask: "Why would this person need to bang his head to get attention?" or even "Does he have so little control over his world that he needs to hurt himself or someone else to gain control?" In the context of a thorough functional analysis, such questions have helped us to use the behavioral technology we have presented in this book in a more creative and, we hope, more humane manner. We exhort you, our readers, to call upon your own creativity and skill in human interaction to do likewise.

Bibliography

Glossary

Index

Bibliography

Positive Programming

Bolstad, O. D., & Johnson, S. M. (1972). Self-regulation in the modification of disruptive classroom behavior. *Journal of Applied Behavior Analysis, 5,* 443–454.

Carr, E. G., & Durand, V. M. (1985). Reducing behavior problems through functional communication training. *Journal of Applied Behavior Analysis, 18,* 111–126.

Donnellan, A. M., & LaVigna, G. W. (1986). Nonaversive control of socially stigmatizing behaviors. *The Pointer, 30*(4), 25–31.

Donnellan, A. M., Mirenda, P. L., Mesaros, R. A., & Fassbender, L. L. (1984). Analyzing the communicative functions of aberrant behavior. *Journal of the Association for the Severely Handicapped, 9*(3), 201–212.

Guess, D., Helmstetter, E., Turnbull, H. R., III, & Knowlton, J. (1987). *Use of aversive procedures with persons who are disabled: An historical review and critical analysis.* Seattle, WA: The Association for Persons with Severe Handicaps.

LaVigna, G. W. (1987). Non-aversive strategies for managing behavior problems. In D. J. Cohen & A. M. Donnellan (Eds.), *Handbook of autism and disorders of atypical development* (pp. 418–429). New York: John Wiley.

LaVigna, G. W., & Donnellan, A. M. (1986). *Alternatives to punishment: Solving behavior problems with non-aversive strategies.* New York: Irvington.

LaVigna, G. W., Willis, T. J., & Donnellan, A. M. (in press). The role of positive programming in non-aversive behavior management. In E. Cipani (Ed.), *Behavioral approaches to the treatment of aberrant behavior* (AAMD Monograph Series). Washington, DC: American Association on Mental Deficiency.

Smith, M. D. (1985). *Working with autism: Strategies for achieving behavioral adjustment at work.* Rockville, MD: Community Services for Autistic Adults and Children.

Smith, M. D. (1986). The use of alternative sensory stimuli in the community-based treatment of the self-stimulatory behavior of an adult disabled by autism. *Journal of Behavior Therapy and Experimental Psychiatry*, *17*, 121–125.

Turnbull, H. R., III, Guess, D., Backus, L. H., Barber, P. A., Fiedler, C. R., Helmstetter, E., & Summers, J. A. (1986). A model for analyzing the moral aspects of special education and behavioral intervention: The moral aspects of aversive procedures. In P. R. Dokecki & R. M. Zaner (Eds.), *Ethics of dealing with persons with severe handicaps: Toward a research agenda* (pp. 167–210). Baltimore, MD: Paul H. Brookes.

Ysseldyke, J. E., & Christenson, S. L. (1987). *The instructional environment scale*. Austin, TX: Pro Ed.

Basic Behavioral Techniques

Baer, D. M., & Sherman, J. A. (1964). Reinforcement control of generalized imitation in young children. *Journal of Experimental Child Psychology*, *1*, 37–49.

Baer, D. M., Wolf, M. M., & Risley, T. R. (1968). Some current dimensions of applied behavior analysis. *Journal of Applied Behavior Analysis*, *1*, 91–97.

Boer, M. (Ed.). (1984). *Investigating the problem of skill generalization: Literature review I*. Seattle, WA: University of Washington.

Evans, I. M., & Meyer, L. H. (1985). *An educative approach to behavior problems: A practical decision model for interventions with severely handicapped learners*. Baltimore: Paul H. Brookes.

Fox, R., Rotatori, A. F., Macklin, F., & Green, H. (1983). Assessing reinforcer preference in severe behaviorally disordered children. *Early Child Development and Care*, *11*, 113–121.

Koegel, R. L., Russo, D. C., & Rincover, A. (1977). Assessing and training teachers in the generalized use of behavior modification with autistic children. *Journal of Applied Behavior Analysis*, *10*, 197–205.

Martin, G., & Pear, J. (1983). *Behavior modification: What it is and how to do it*. Englewood Cliffs, NJ: Prentice-Hall.

Project TEACCH (1980). *Nothing is rewarding to this child*. Piedmont Teaching Center, University of North Carolina, Chapel Hill.

Sulzer, B., & Mayer, G. R. (1972). *Behavior modification procedures for school personnel*. Hinsdale, IL: Dryden Press.

Teaching Technology

Baer, D. M. (1981). *How to plan for generalization*. Lawrence, KS: H & H Enterprises.

Cautela, J. R., & Brion-Meisels, L. (1979). A children's reinforcement survey schedule. *Psychological Reports*, *44*, 327–338.

Donnellan-Walsh, A. M., Gossage, L. D., LaVigna, G. W., Schuler, A. L., & Traphagen, J. (1976). *Teaching makes a difference: A guide for developing successful classes for autistic and other severely handicapped children — Teacher's manual*. Sacramento, CA: California State Department of Education.

Favell, J. E. (1977). *The power of positive reinforcement: A handbook of behavior modification*. Springfield, IL: Charles C Thomas.

Harris, F. R., Johnston, M. K., Kelly, C. S., & Wolf, M. M. (1964). Effects of positive social reinforcement on regressed crawling of a nursery school child. *Journal of Educational Psychology, 55*, 35–41.

Harris, F. R., Wolf, M. M., & Baer, D. M. (1964). Effects of adult social reinforcement on child behavior. *Young Children, 20*(1), 8–17.

Koegel, R. L., Egel, A. L., & Dunlap, G. (1980). Learning characteristics of autistic children. In W. Sailor, B. Wilcox, & L. Brown (Eds.), *Methods of instruction for severely handicapped students* (pp. 259–301). Baltimore: Paul H. Brookes.

Koegel, R. L., Rincover, A., & Egel, A. L. (1982). *Educating and understanding autistic children*. San Diego: College Hill Press.

Premack, D. (1959). Toward empirical behavior laws: I. Positive reinforcement. *Psychological Review, 66*, 219–233.

Woods, T. S. (1987). The technology of instruction: A behavior analytic approach. In D. J. Cohen & A. M. Donnellan (Eds.), *Handbook of autism and disorders of atypical development* (pp. 251–272). New York: John Wiley.

Data Collection

Repp, A. C., Roberts, D. M., Slack, D. J., Repp, C. F., & Berkler, M. S. (1976). A comparison of frequency, interval, and time-sampling methods of data collection. *Journal of Applied Behavior Analysis, 9*, 501–508.

Touchette, P. E., MacDonald, R. F., & Langer, S. N. (1985). A scatter plot for identifying stimulus control of problem behavior. *Journal of Applied Behavior Analysis, 18*, 343–351.

Prompts and Prompt Fading

Billingsley, F. F., & Romer, L. T. (1983). Response prompting and the transfer of stimulus control: Methods, research, and a conceptual framework. *Journal of the Association for the Severely Handicapped, 8*(2), 3–12.

Csapo, M. (1981). Comparison of two prompting procedures to increase response fluency among severely handicapped learners. *Journal of the Association for the Severely Handicapped, 6*(1), 39–47.

Donnellan, A. M., & Mirenda, P. L. (1983). A model for analyzing instructional components to facilitate generalization for severely handicapped students. *Journal of Special Education, 17*, 317–331.

Falvey, M., Brown, L., Lyon, S., Baumgart, D., & Schroeder, J. (1980). Strategies for using cues and correction procedures. In W. Sailor, B. Wilcox, & L. Brown (Eds.), *Methods of instruction for severely handicapped students* (pp. 109–133). Baltimore, MD: Paul H. Brookes.

Gold, M. (1974). Redundant cue removal in skill training for the mildly and moderately retarded. *Education and Training of the Mentally Retarded*, 9, 5–8.

Koegel, R. L., & Rincover, A. (1976). Some detrimental effects of using extra stimuli to guide learning in normal and autistic children. *Journal of Abnormal Child Psychology*, 4, 59–71.

Mahoney, K., Van Wagenen, R. K., & Meyerson, L. (1971). Toilet training of normal and retarded children. *Journal of Applied Behavior Analysis*, 4, 173–181.

Mesaros, R. A. (1982). *An analysis of prompt dependency in an autistic adolescent.* Unpublished manuscript, University of Wisconsin-Madison.

Nelson, D. L., Gergenti, E., & Hollander, A. C. (1980). Extra prompts versus no extra prompts in self-care training of autistic children and adolescents. *Journal of Autism and Developmental Disorders*, 10, 311–321.

Schreibman, L. (1975). Effects of within-stimulus and extra-stimulus prompting on discrimination learning in autistic children. *Journal of Applied Behavior Analysis*, 8, 91–112.

Alt-R

Allen, K. E., Hart, B. M., Buell, J. S., Harris, F. R., & Wolf, M. M. (1964). Effects of social reinforcement on isolate behavior of a nursery school child. *Child Development*, 35, 511–518.

Hall, R. V., Lund, D., & Jackson, D. (1968). Effects of teacher attention on study behavior. *Journal of Applied Behavior Analysis*, 1, 1–12.

Hawkins, R. P., Peterson, R. F., Schweid, E., & Bijou, S. W. (1966). Behavior therapy in the home: Amelioration of problem parent-child relations with the parent in a therapeutic role. *Journal of Experimental Child Psychology*, 4, 99–107.

LeBlanc, J. M., Reuter, K. E., Miller, D. N., & Schilmoeller, G. L. (1977). Laboratory investigations of applied behavior analysis techniques: Procedures designed to decrease or eliminate responding. In B. C. Etzel, J. M. LeBlanc, & D. M. Baer (Eds.), *New developments in behavioral research: Theory, method, and application* (pp. 189–229). Hillsdale, NJ: Lawrence Erlbaum.

O'Leary, K. D., O'Leary, S., & Becker, W. C. (1967). Modification of a deviant sibling interaction pattern in the home. *Behaviour Research and Therapy*, 5, 113–120.

Russo, S. (1964). Adaptations in behavioral therapy with children. *Behaviour Research and Therapy*, 2, 43–47.

Young, J. A., & Wincze, J. P. (1974). The effects of the reinforcement of compatible and incompatible alternative behaviors on the self-injurious and related behaviors of a profoundly retarded female adult. *Behavior Therapy*, 5, 614–623.

DRO

Ball, T. S., McCrady, R. E., & Teixeira, J. (1978). Automated monitoring and cuing for positive reinforcement and differential reinforcement of other behavior. *Journal of Behavior Therapy and Experimental Psychiatry*, 9, 33–37.

Deitz, S. M., Repp, A. C., & Deitz, D. E. D. (1976). Reducing inappropriate classroom behavior of retarded students through three procedures of differential reinforcement. *Journal of Mental Deficiency Research, 20*, 155–170.

Homer, A. L., & Peterson, L. (1980). Differential reinforcement of other behavior: A preferred response elimination procedure. *Behavior Therapy, 11*, 449–471.

Lowitz, G. H., & Suib, M. R. (1978). Generalized control of persistent thumbsucking by differential reinforcement of other behaviors. *Journal of Behavior Therapy and Experimental Psychiatry, 9*, 343–346.

Luiselli, J. K., Helfen, C. S., Colozzi, G., Donellon, S., & Pemberton, B. (1978). Controlling the self-inflicted biting of a retarded child by the differential reinforcement of other behavior. *Psychological Reports, 42*, 435–438.

Peterson, R. F., & Peterson, L. R. (1968). The use of positive reinforcement in the control of self-destructive behavior in a retarded boy. *Journal of Experimental Child Psychology, 6*, 351–360.

Repp, A. C., Deitz, S. M., & Deitz, D. E. D. (1976). Reducing inappropriate behaviors in classrooms and in individual sessions through DRO schedules of reinforcement. *Mental Retardation, 14*(1), 11–15.

Repp, A. C., Deitz, S. M., & Speir, N. C. (1974). Reducing stereotypic responding of retarded persons by the differential reinforcement of other behavior. *American Journal of Mental Deficiency, 79*, 279–284.

Repp, A. C., & Slack, D. J. (1977). Reducing responding of retarded persons by DRO schedules following a history of low-rate responding: A comparison of ascending interval sizes. *Psychological Records, 27*, 581–588.

Reynolds, G. S. (1961). Behavioral contrast. *Journal of the Experimental Analysis of Behavior, 4*, 57–71.

Topping, J. S., Graves, A. J., & Moss, J. D. (1975). Response elimination in elementary and special education school children. *Psychological Record, 25*, 567–572.

Weiher, R. G., & Harman, R. E. (1975). The use of omission training to reduce self-injurious behavior in a retarded child. *Behavior Therapy, 6*, 261–268.

DRL

Bolstad, O. D., & Johnson, S. M. (1972). Self-regulation in the modification of disruptive classroom behavior. *Journal of Applied Behavior Analysis, 5*, 443–454.

Carter, D. E., & Bruno, L. J. J. (1968). Extinction and reconditioning of behavior generated by a DRL contingency of reinforcement. *Psychonomic Science, 11*, 19–20.

Deitz, S. M., & Repp, A. C. (1973). Decreasing classroom misbehavior through the use of DRL schedules of reinforcement. *Journal of Applied Behavior Analysis, 6*, 457–463.

Deitz, S. M., & Repp, A. C. (1974). Differentially reinforcing low rates of misbehavior with normal elementary school children. *Journal of Applied Behavior Analysis, 7*, 622.

Kapostins, E. E. (1963). The effects of DRL schedules on some characteristics of word utterance. *Journal of the Experimental Analysis of Behavior, 6,* 281–290.

Kramer, T. J., & Rilling, M. (1970). Differential reinforcement of low rates: A selective critique. *Psychological Bulletin, 74,* 225–254.

Stimulus Control

Epstein, L. H., Peterson, G. L., Webster, J., Guanieri, C., & Libby, B. (1973). Comparison of stimulus control and reinforcement control effects on imitative behavior. *Journal of Experimental Child Psychology, 16,* 98–110.

Huguenin, N. H., & Touchette, P. E. (1980). Visual attention in retarded adults: Combining stimuli which control incompatible behavior. *Journal of the Experimental Analysis of Behavior, 33,* 77–86.

Rincover, A., & Koegel, R. L. (1975). Setting generality and stimulus control in autistic children. *Journal of Applied Behavior Analysis, 8,* 235–246.

Rollings, J. P., & Baumeister, A. A. (1981). Stimulus control of stereotypic responding: Effects on target and collateral behavior. *American Journal of Mental Deficiency, 86,* 67–77.

Sailor, W., Guess, D., Rutherford, G., & Baer, D. M. (1968). Control of tantrum behavior by operant techniques during experimental verbal training. *Journal of Applied Behavior Analysis, 1,* 237–243.

Spradlin, J. E., Cotter, V. W., & Baxley, N. (1973). Establishing a conditional discrimination without direct training: A study of transfer with retarded adolescents. *American Journal of Mental Deficiency, 77,* 556–566.

Touchette, P. E. (1968). The effects of graduated stimulus change on the acquisition of a simple discrimination in severely retarded boys. *Journal of the Experimental Analysis of Behavior, 11,* 39–48.

Instructional Control

Engelmann, S., & Colvin, W. (1983). *Generalized compliance training: A direct-instruction program for managing severe behavior problems.* Eugene, OR: E-B Press.

Etzel, B. C., & LeBlanc, J. M. (1979). The simplest treatment alternative: The law of parsimony applied to choosing appropriate instructional control and error-less-learning procedures for the difficult-to-teach child. *Journal of Autism and Developmental Disorders, 9,* 361–382.

Homme, L. E., Csanyi, A. P., Gonzales, M. A., & Rechs, J. R. (1969). *How to use contingency contracting in the classroom.* Champaign, IL: Research Press.

Kazdin, A. E., & Erickson, L. M. (1975). Developing responsiveness to instructions in severely and profoundly retarded residents. *Journal of Behavior Therapy and Experimental Psychiatry, 6,* 17–21.

Russo, D. C., Cataldo, M. F., & Cushing, P. J. (1981). Compliance training and behavioral covariation in the treatment of multiple behavior problems. *Journal of Applied Behavior Analysis, 14,* 209–222.

Sailor, W., Guess, D., Rutherford, G., & Baer, D. M. (1968). Control of tantrum behavior by operant techniques during experimental verbal training. *Journal of Applied Behavior Analysis, 1*, 237–243.

Striefel, S., & Wetherby, B. (1973). Instruction-following behavior of a retarded child and its controlling stimuli. *Journal of Applied Behavior Analysis, 6*, 663–670.

Volkmar, F. R., & Cohen, D. J. (1982). A hierarchical analysis of patterns of noncompliance in autistic and behavior-disturbed children. *Journal of Autism and Developmental Disorders, 12*, 35–42.

Whitman, T. L., Zakaras, M., & Chardos, S. (1971). Effects of reinforcement and guidance procedures on instruction-following behavior of severely retarded children. *Journal of Applied Behavior Analysis, 4*, 283–290.

Stimulus Change

Azrin, N. H. (1958). Some effects of noise on human behavior. *Journal of the Experimental Analysis of Behavior, 1*, 183–200.

Goldiamond, I. (1965). Self-control procedures in personal behavior problems. *Psychological Reports, 17*, 851–868.

LaVigna, G. W., & Donnellan-Walsh, A. M. (1976). *Alternatives to the use of punishment in the school setting.* Paper presented at the Eighth Annual Southern California Conference on Behavior Modification, California State University, Los Angeles.

Stimulus Satiation

Axelrod, S., Brantner, J. P., & Meddock, T. D. (1978). Overcorrection: A review and critical analysis. *Journal of Special Education, 12*, 367–491.

Ayllon, T. (1963). Intensive treatment of psychotic behavior by stimulus satiation and food reinforcement. *Behaviour Research and Therapy, 1*, 53–61.

Blackman, G. J., & Silberman, A. (1971). *Modification of child behavior.* Belmont, CA: Wadsworth.

Shaping

Cuvo, A. J., Veitch, V. D., Trace, M. W., & Konke, J. L. (1978). Teaching change computation to the mentally retarded. *Behavior Modification, 2*, 531–548.

Humphreys, L., Forehand, R., Cheney, T., & Adams, S. V. (1977). Training retarded individuals in communication skills: An experimental program. *Journal of Clinical Child Psychology, 6*, 33–37.

Reich, R. (1978). Gestural facilitation of expressive language in moderately/severely retarded preschoolers. *Mental Retardation, 16*, 113–117.

Song, A. Y., & Gandhi, R. (1974). An analysis of behavior during the acquisition and maintenance phases of self-spoon feeding skills of profound retardates. *Mental Retardation, 12*(1), 25–28.

Song, A. Y., Song, R. H., & Grant, P. A. (1976). Toilet training in the school and its transfer in the living unit. *Journal of Behavior Therapy and Experimental Psychiatry, 7*, 281–284.

Stone, M. C. (1970). Behavior shaping in a classroom for children with cerebral palsy. *Exceptional Children, 36*, 674–677.

Wehman, P., Karan, O., & Rettie, C. (1976). Developing independent play in three severely retarded women. *Psychological Reports, 39*, 995–998.

Additive Procedures

Berkman, K. A., & Meyer, L. H. (in press). Alternative strategies and multiple outcomes in the remediation of severe self injury: Going "all out" nonaversively. *Journal of the Association for Persons with Severe Handicaps.*

Bondy, A. S., & Erickson, M. T. (1976). Comparison of modelling and reinforcement procedures in increasing question-asking of mildly retarded children. *Journal of Applied Behavior Analysis, 9*, 108.

Peterson, R. F., & Peterson, L. R. (1968). The use of positive reinforcement in the control of self-destructive behavior in a retarded boy. *Journal of Experimental Child Psychology, 6*, 351–360.

Zimmerman, E. H., & Zimmerman, J. (1962). The alteration of behavior in a special classroom situation. *Journal of the Experimental Analysis of Behavior, 5*, 59–60.

Crisis and Intervention Strategies

N.A.P.P.I. (1985). *Non-abusive physical and psychological intervention.* Auburn, ME: Author, 250 Minot Avenue.

Palotai, A., Mance, A., & Negri, N. A. (1982). *Averting and handling aggressive behavior.* Columbia, SC: South Carolina Department of Mental Health.

Willis, T. J., & LaVigna, G. W. (1983). *Emergency management guidelines.* Los Angeles: Institute for Applied Behavior Analysis, 1840 Imperial Highway.

Zivolich, S., & Thvedt, J. (1983). *Assault crisis training: Prevention and intervention.* Huntington Beach, CA: Special Education Counseling Service.

Curriculum Development and Adaptations

Baumgart, D., Brown, L., Pumpian, I., Nisbet, J., Ford, A., Sweet, M., Messina, R., & Schroeder, J. (1982). Principle of partial participation and individualized adaptations in educational programs for severely handicapped students. *Journal of the Association for the Severely Handicapped, 7*(2), 17–27.

Brown, L., Nietupski, J., & Hamre-Nietupski, S. (1976). The criterion of ultimate functioning and public school services for severely handicapped students. In M. A. Thomas (Ed.), *Hey, don't forget about me: Education's investment in the severely, profoundly, and multiply handicapped* (pp. 2-15). Reston, VA: Council for Exceptional Children.

Cooke, T. P., & Apolloni, T. (1976). Developing positive social-emotional behaviors: A study of training and generalization effects. *Journal of Applied Behavior Analysis, 9,* 65-78.

Donnellan, A. M. (1980). An educational perspective of autism: Implications for curriculum development and personnel development. In B. Wilcox & A. Thompson (Eds.), *Critical issues in educating autistic children and youth* (pp. 53-88). Washington, DC: U.S. Department of Education, Office of Special Education.

Edgar, E., Maser, J., Smith, D., & Haring, N. G. (1977). Developing an instructional sequence for teaching a self-help skill. *Education and Training of the Mentally Retarded, 12*(1), 42-51.

Ford, A., Brown, L., Pumpian, I., Baumgart, D., Nisbet, J., Schroeder, J., & Loomis, R. (1980). Strategies for developing individualized recreation/leisure plans for adolescent and young adult severely handicapped students. In L. Brown, M. Falvey, I. Pumpian, D. Baumgart, J. Nisbet, A. Ford, J. Schroeder, & R. Loomis (Eds.), *Curricular strategies for teaching severely handicapped students functional skills in school and non-school environments* (Vol. X, pp. 14-151). Madison, WI: University of Wisconsin-Madison and Madison Metropolitan School District.

Ford, A., & Mirenda, P. (1984). Community instruction: A natural cues and consequences decision model. *Journal of the Association for Persons with Severe Handicaps, 9,* 79-87.

Meyer, L. H., & Evans, I. M. (1985). Modification of excess behavior: An adaptive and functional approach for educational and community contexts. In R. H. Horner, L. H. Meyer, & H. D. Fredericks (Eds.), *Education of learners with severe handicaps: Exemplary service strategies* (pp. 12-66). Baltimore: Paul H. Brookes.

Mirenda, P., & Donnellan, A. M. (1987). Issues in curriculum development. In D. J. Cohen & A. M. Donnellan (Eds.), *Handbook of autism and disorders of atypical development* (pp. 211-226). New York: John Wiley.

Wehman, P., Schleien, S., & Kiernan, J. (1980). Age appropriate recreation programs for severely handicapped youth and adults. *Journal of the Association for the Severely Handicapped, 5,* 395-407.

Williams, W. W. (1975). Procedures of task analysis as related to developing instructional programs for the severely handicapped. In L. Brown, T. Crowner, W. Williams, & R. York (Eds.), *Madison alternative to zero exclusion: A book of readings.* Madison, WI: Madison Metropolitan School District.

Glossary

Additive procedure   The combination of two or more procedures to manage a behavior problem.

Alternative response   The replacement for the target behavior.

Alt-R   See *differential reinforcement of alternative behaviors*.

Anecdotal recording   A method of descriptively recording learner response, the response of others, and information about the environment. The information should be described as objectively as possible.

Aversive stimulus

> **Unconditioned aversive stimulus**   A type of stimulus that results in physical pain or discomfort to the student.

> **Conditioned aversive stimulus**   A type of stimulus that a person learns to experience as aversive as a result of its being paired with an unconditioned aversive stimulus.

Backward chaining   A procedure that involves teaching a complete sequence of behaviors that must be performed in a particular order, starting with the last step and working backward to the first.

Baseline data   Data that reflect the level of occurrence of behavior before intervention.

Chaining   A procedure that involves teaching a complete sequence of behaviors that must be performed in a particular order. Also see *backward chaining*, *forward chaining*, and *global chaining*.

Consequence (C)   An environmental stimulus or event that contingently follows the occurrence of a particular response and, as a result of that contingency relationship, strengthens or weakens the future occurrence of that response.

Contingent withdrawal   The removal of a reinforcer or other stimulus, contingent upon the occurrence of a specified behavior.

Continuous reinforcement (CRF) schedule   A schedule of reinforcement under which every response is reinforced. This schedule builds behavior rapidly.

Correction procedure   The assistance provided to a learner *after* an incorrect response is given. It is sometimes referred to as a postresponse prompt.

Differential reinforcement   Reinforcement given only when a certain response occurs, possibly only in the presence of a given stimulus or a group of stimuli which then becomes discriminative for the response.

Differential reinforcement of alternative behaviors (Alt-R; also DRA)   The differential reinforcement of specified behaviors that are topographically different from the target behavior. This procedure is also called the *differential reinforcement of incompatible behaviors* (DRI) and *the differential reinforcement of competing behaviors* (DRC).

Differential reinforcement of low rates of responding (DRL)   Reinforcement of low rates of responding, either following a specified interval since the previous response, or after a specified interval if the rate is below a specified criterion.

Differential reinforcement of other behaviors (DRO)   Reinforcement for not engaging in the target behavior for a specified interval of time.

Discrete-trial format (DTF)   A teaching format that has clearly discriminable steps, as follows: stimulus→response→consequence.

Discriminative stimulus (S^D)   An environmental stimulus, cue, or event that sets the occasion for a particular response by indicating the availability of a particular consequence.

DRL   See *differential reinforcement of low rates of responding.*

DRL-IRT   A variation of DRL in which the response is reinforced if it follows a specified interval since the previous response.

DRO   See *differential reinforcement of other behaviors.*

DRO fixed-interval schedule   A procedure in which the interval schedule is fixed and reinforcement is delivered at the end of each interval, if the response has not occurred.

DRO progressive schedule (DROP)   A procedure in which the interval size remains the same and the amount and/or kind of reinforcement increases as the student passes through consecutive intervals without performing the undesirable behavior.

DRO reset schedules   A procedure in which the interval timer is reset each time the response or target behavior occurs.

Duration recording   A data recording technique that measures the total time (out of a designated time period) that an individual is engaged in a particular response.

Event recording   A data recording technique in which a cumulative record of discrete responses is collected.

Extinction   The withholding of a previously available consequence for a response, which results in a decrease or weakening of response rate, duration, or intensity.

Fixed-interval (FI) schedule An intermittent schedule of reinforcement in which reinforcement opportunity occurs after a fixed amount of time.

Fixed-ratio (FR) schedule An intermittent schedule of reinforcement where a reinforcer is given after a specified number of times that a behavior occurs.

Forward chaining A procedure of teaching behaviors beginning with the first behavior required by the task, then the second, third, fourth, and so on.

Free access A condition of unlimited access to a reinforcer, used to determine the maximum quantity of that reinforcer a person would ordinarily choose.

Functional analysis An analysis of the factors that affect a particular behavior including a thorough assessment of the following: (1) the events that follow behavior (consequence), (2) the events that precede behavior (discriminative and instructional-abstractional variables), (3) events that prop up behavior (ecological or stimulus props), (4) the history of the behavior, and (5) the procedures that provide change (programs).

Generalization The process of transferring a learned behavior to different but related stimulus environments; that is, the expansion of a student's capability to perform the task beyond those conditions set for initial acquisition which may include instructional cues, materials, or formats; people; and environments (settings).

Global chaining The process of teaching component parts of a task, then chaining them together. Global chaining, whether in a whole-task or step-by-step presentation, can start at the beginning, end, or middle of the sequence, depending on which steps of the task are easiest. It is also possible to move within the sequence of steps, such as from 1 to 4, then on to 6, and so forth.

Inadvertent reinforcement The unintentional reinforcement of behaviors.

Increasing-interval schedule A variation of a DRO procedure in which the interval size between responses is gradually increased. The reinforcer is delivered at the end of the specified interval, if the target response has not occurred.

Instructional control An instance of stimulus control when a response occurs in the presence of or following the presentation of a command, direction, request, or verbal cue (spoken, written, or otherwise).

Intermittent reinforcement schedule A schedule of reinforcement under which some but not all occurrences of a behavior are reinforced. Intermittent schedules of reinforcement maintain behaviors.

Interresponse time (IRT)   The interval of time between occurrences of the target behavior.

Intertrial interval   The period of time between the end of a teaching trial and the initiation of another; used to provide a clear beginning and ending, as well as possibly time for recording data and/or more informal social interaction.

Limited hold   Withholding of the reinforcer for a short period of time after the occurrence of the correct response.

Negative reinforcement   A situation that occurs when the contingent removal of a certain stimulus or event results in a future increase or strengthening, over time, of response rate, duration, or intensity. Also see *positive reinforcement*, below.

100% rule   Defining the target behavior and the alternative responses so that, together, by definition, they cover the universe of possibilities; that is, the learner can either engage in the target behavior or in the alternative response(s), with no third option.

Physical prompt   A prompt that involves direct physical guidance of the learner; *not* forced responding. Also see *prompt*.

Positive programming   A gradual educational process for behavior change, based on a functional analysis of the presenting problems and involving systematic instruction in more effective ways of behaving.

Positive reinforcement   A situation that occurs when the contingent presentation of a certain stimulus or event results in a future increase or strengthening, over time, of response rate, duration, or intensity.

Pragmatic analysis   A systematic analysis of behavior in relation to the context in which it occurs, in order to determine its communication value.

Prompt   Assistance provided to a learner after the presentation of the instructional stimulus but *before* the response, to assure a correct response; sometimes referred to as a preresponse prompt.

Prompt fading   The systematic reduction of a prompt until it is eliminated or becomes part of the task.

Rebound   The phenomenon of a behavior returning, after contingencies are discontinued, to a level that is higher than its preintervention level.

Recovery   The phenomenon of a behavior returning to preintervention levels, once contingencies are no longer in effect.

Reinforcement frequency   How often a reinforcer is delivered.

Reinforcing stimulus   A stimulus or event that, when contingently presented after a response, results in a future increase of that response.

Reset schedule   A schedule of reinforcement in which the occurrence of the behavior causes the reinforcement timer to be reset.

Response (R)   Observable, measurable behavior.

Response class   A group of behaviors that as a group are affected by contingencies applied to any member of that group.

S$^\triangle$(S-delta)   Those stimuli that signal the nonavailability of reinforcement for a particular response.

S^D   See *discriminative stimulus*.

Scatter-plot recording   A method for collecting and/or graphing behavioral data by date and time of a behavioral occurrence across a number of environmental variables. This allows for some visual analysis of behavior changes as a function of environmental events.

Schedule of reinforcement   The predetermined time period or rate at which reinforcement is delivered or withheld for a given behavior, used to dictate the characteristics of the response.

Shaping   The gradual modification and differential reinforcement of successive approximations to a desired behavior.

Social validation   The general acceptability of treatment goals and procedures.

Stimulus change   The sudden and noncontingent introduction of a new stimulus or a dramatic alteration of the stimulus conditions, which results in a temporary period of target response reduction.

Stimulus control   The discriminative control of a behavior resulting from reinforcing that behavior in the presence of a certain stimulus; the behavior then becomes more likely to occur in the presence of the stimulus, and less likely in its absence.

Stimulus satiation   The continuous and noncontingent availability of an identified reinforcer that is maintaining an undesired behavior, thereby weakening the reinforcer's effectiveness and reducing the rate of the defined behavior.

Tangible reinforcers   Objects that have reinforcing value, such as tokens, tickets, or marbles.

Target behavior   The specific response that has been identified to be either increased or decreased.

Target behavior occurrence   An occurrence of the behavior identified as the one to be increased or decreased.

Time sampling   A direct observational method of recording data in which the observer records, in short intervals, the presence or absence of the behavior(s) to be changed.

Topographic compatibility   A condition wherein one response is physically compatible with another, such that it is physically possible to perform both at the same time, for example, working with one's hands and making noises.

Topographic dissimilarity   A condition wherein one response is physically different from another, for example, combing one's hair and catching a ball.

Topographic incompatibility   A condition wherein one response is physically incompatible with another, such that it is physically impossible to perform both at the same time, for example, sitting down and standing up.

Topographic similarity   A condition wherein one response is physically similar to another, for example, poking people and touching them gently.

Topography of behavior   The physical qualities of a behavior; what it looks like.

Trial-by-trial data   Data that are recorded at the end of each discrete trial, indicating if the response was correct, incorrect, correctly prompted, or incorrectly prompted.

Type I punishment   The contingent presentation of a stimulus or event which results in a *future decrease* or weakening of response rate, duration, or intensity.

Type II punishment   The contingent withdrawal of a stimulus or event which results in a *future decrease* or weakening of response rate, duration, or intensity.

Variable-interval (VI) schedule   An intermittent schedule of reinforcement in which reinforcement becomes available after the passage of variable intervals of time.

Variable-ratio (VR) schedule   An intermittent schedule of reinforcement in which reinforcement becomes available after a variable number of responses are made, with the variation revolving around a certain fixed average number of responses.

Visual prompt   A prompt that involves the use of something visual, such as gestures, pictures, demonstration or modeling, or written signs.

Within-stimulus prompt   A prompt in which a relevant part or dimension of the task is exaggerated initially, such as proximity, color, shape, or volume.

Index